CW00321907

LITTLE BOOK OF

Great
EXPLORERS

LITTLE BOOK OF

Great
EXPLORERS

First published in the UK in 2014

© Demand Media Limited 2014

www.demand-media.co.uk

Printed and bound in Europe

ISBN 978-1-910270-17-2

Contents

Introduction

From our earliest ancestors to men and women like Ferdinand Magellan and Amelia Earhart, our appetite for knowledge and discovery via exploration has been insatiable. We have now explored just about every square inch of the surface of our planet and – thanks to Jacques Cousteau, Jacques Piccard and Don Walsh – a good deal of what lies beneath the seas. We have also visited the Moon and sent probes deep into the cosmos.

From Marco Polo, Christopher Columbus and Captain James Cook to Roald Amundsen, Sir Edmund Hillary, Neil Armstrong, Amy Johnson and Sir Ranulph Fiennes, we look at the extraordinary lives of the pioneers and adventurers who discovered peoples and places as remote and wondrous as any on Earth.

With Mars likely to be visited by the next generation of space travellers, now is the time to celebrate the achievements of our greatest explorers.

Roald Amundsen

Roald Amundsen was born in Borge, Norway, to Jens Amundsen and Hanna Sahlqvist in July 1872. The family had all been seafarers but Hanna encouraged Roald to become a doctor rather than pursue a dangerous occupation in the navy. He resisted the temptation to explore the world's wildernesses – a boyhood passion – until his mother passed away when he was 21.

In 1897 Amundsen joined the Belgian Antarctic Expedition sailing on the *Belgica*. When it became trapped in ice off the Antarctic Peninsula, the crew became the first to endure a southern winter. Although they were poorly prepared, the doctor insisted they hunt for fresh seal meat to ward off scurvy. This undoubtedly saved their lives and it was valuable lesson in polar exploration for Amundsen.

While making the first traverse of the Northwest Passage between 1903 and 1906, Amundsen learned more invaluable survival skills from the Netsilik people, including how to use sled dogs to transport loads, as well as how to fashion protective clothing from animal hide.

Three years later, Amundsen cancelled a proposed trip to the North Pole because Americans Robert Peary and Frederick Cook both claimed to have got there first (both would later have doubt cast upon their assertions). Instead, Amundsen headed to Antarctica to try to reach the South Pole even though he knew Captain Robert Scott was also making an attempt.

His ship, the *Fram*, reached the Bay of Whales in January 1911. Having established a base camp, Amundsen used dogs to ferry supplies to depots on the ice cap. A first expedition to the pole itself

had to turn back due to extreme cold but Amundsen then led a second party, which left base camp in October. His five-man team used four sleds and 52 dogs to navigate the uncharted Axel Heiberg Glacier and the polar plateau.

After a largely uneventful two-month trek across the ice, the team reached the South Pole on December 14th. They all returned safely to base by the end of January 1912 but they couldn't announce their success to the wider world until they

reached Hobart, Tasmania, in March. There is no doubt that Amundsen's success was down to preparation, equipment, clothing, tactics and an understanding of how the dogs could tow sleds and men on skis. He also wasted no time surveying the terrain or taking photographs or other astronomical measurements.

In 1918 Amundsen led an expedition to chart the Northeast Passage to the north of Scandinavia and Russia as far as the Bering Strait. His ship became trapped

LITTLE BOOK OF **GREAT EXPLORERS**

in the ice for two years and it wasn't until 1921 that he reached Seattle to make repairs. Five years later, Amundsen made the first Arctic crossing by air in the airship *Norge*. As Peary and Cook's claims to have reached the pole are still in dispute, as is Richard Byrd's effort in a Fokker Tri-motor a few days earlier, Amundsen could well be the first person to have reached the North Pole. (The first people to step foot on the ice at the pole were probably Russian geophysicists Mikhail Ostrekin and Pavel Senko, and oceanographers Mikhail Somov and Pavel Gordienko, although they still flew there on a science mission rather than trekked overland. If Peary and Cook's claims can't be verified, then the first expedition to reach the pole overland probably wasn't until Ralph Plaisted's in April 1968.)

Amundsen's plane disappeared in 1928 while on a mission to rescue the crew of the airship *Italia*, which had crashed on its return journey from the North Pole. Although wreckage was recovered near the Tromsø coast in the Barents Sea, Amundsen and the crew were never found. He left an enormous body of work and was honoured by having mountains, glaciers and other polar features named after him.

Neil Armstrong, Buzz Aldrin & Michael Collins

Neil Armstrong was born in Ohio in August 1930 to Stephen and Viola. The family travelled for much of his youth and Armstrong became interested in flying when his father took him to Cleveland Air Races. When he was five, he and Stephen took a short flight in a Ford Trimotor.

Armstrong went to Blume High School and spent every spare minute learning to fly at Wapakoneta Airfield. Indeed he ended up with a pilot's licence before he could drive a car. At 17, Armstrong enrolled at Purdue University to study aeronautical engineering. Although he was then accepted to MIT, he was persuaded to stay at Purdue and he graduated in 1955.

During his time at college he also enlisted with the navy at their air station in Pensacola. By 1950 he was a qualified naval aviator, and the following year he saw action in the Korean War. He was shot down while making a bombing run but managed to eject safely and eventually flew 78 sorties. He remained with the reserve for another eight years, during which time he became a trusted research pilot.

In 1956 he helped land a stricken B-29 after one of its propellers disintegrated and damaged the other engines, and he then experienced nose-wheel failure when landing a Bell X-1 rocket plane. He also took an experimental X-15 to an altitude of 63 kilometres. Two years later he applied for the US's space program and was accepted. He was then chosen to command *Gemini 8*, although the mission ran into trouble and had to re-enter the Earth's atmosphere before its objectives were complete.

In early 1967 Armstrong and his fellow Apollo astronauts were told that they would form the nucleus of the crews that would go to the Moon. He was initially named as backup to *Apollo 9*, an Earth-orbit test mission, but, after delays and reassignments, he was given command of *Apollo 11*. While testing the lunar landing training vehicle (nicknamed the flying bedstead), Armstrong lost control

and ejected moments before it crashed.

By March 1969 Armstrong, Buzz Aldrin and Michael Collins had been selected to be the first crew to land on the Moon. As mission leader, Armstrong would take the first steps on the lunar surface (the fact that he didn't have much of an ego, and the way the hatch opened meant he had to be first out, were also considered when making the decision).

Edwin 'Buzz' Aldrin was born to Edwin Senior and Marion Moon in New Jersey in January 1930. He left Montclair High School in 1946 but then turned down a scholarship to MIT in favour of entering West Point Military Academy in New York. He graduated with a degree in mechanical engineering and, like Armstrong, then served as a pilot in the Korean War.

He flew several experimental aircraft before becoming an aerial gunnery instructor. In 1963 he earned a doctorate in astronautics from MIT, specifically line-of-sight guidance for orbital rendezvous. He was then assigned to the Air Force Space Division in Los Angeles before applying to serve as an astronaut.

After the deaths of the *Gemini 9* crew, he took command of the next mission.

He also set a record for extra-vehicular activity (EVA) during the *Gemini 12* mission, proving that astronauts could work outside their spacecraft for extended periods. In early 1969, he too was assigned to *Apollo 11*.

Michael Collins was born in Rome in October 1930 to Major-General James Collins and his wife Virginia. The family travelled for most of the first 17 years of his life but he found time to attend St Albans School in Washington. Rather than enter the diplomatic service, he chose to enrol in a military academy and then joined the air force.

He had to eject from an F-86 during a NATO exercise in 1956 because of a fire, so he then diversified into aircraft maintenance. He applied to become a test pilot at Edwards Air Force Base in 1960 and was subsequently chosen for fighter operations. When he heard about John Glen's historic *Mercury* space flight, he applied to become an astronaut but his first attempt was unsuccessful. In May 1963 he reapplied and was accepted.

Two years later, Collins was chosen as backup for *Gemini 7* and then to the main crew of *Gemini 10*. He performed his first EVA on the mission in 1966 and he was then assigned to the Apollo Space Program. He was meant to join the crew of *Apollo 9* but he had to have back surgery on herniated discs and ended up as capsule communicator for *Apollo 8*, the first mission to complete a successful lunar orbit. Having recovered from surgery, Collins was chosen as command module pilot for *Apollo 11*.

On July 16th 1969, millions of people around the world watched as a Saturn V rocket blasted into the sky from the Kennedy Space Center in Florida. After completing one and a half Earth orbits, a trans-lunar injection burn sent the command/service module on its way to the Moon. Three days later, *Apollo 11* entered lunar orbit. On July 20th the lunar module *Eagle* carrying Armstrong and Aldrin separated from Collins in the command module, *Columbia*.

The *Eagle* began its descent but the crew were soon distracted by computer alarms. Having deemed them not serious, and with Aldrin calling out navigational data, Armstrong brought the lander down onto the lunar surface. Although they first confirmed the contact and then went through a checklist, Armstrong finally announced: "Houston, Tranquillity Base here. The *Eagle* has landed."

Opposite: *Buzz Aldrin and Jim Lovell celebrate a safe return to Earth after the Gemini 12 mission*

He and Aldrin were then supposed to catch up on some sleep but they were so excited that they prepared for the moonwalk instead. Six and a half hours after touching down on the Moon, 600 million people on Earth watched grainy television pictures as Neil Armstrong exited the hatch and climbed down the ladder. As he set foot on the Moon, he said: "That's one small step for man, one giant leap for mankind."

A few moments later, Aldrin joined him, describing the view as "Magnificent desolation." He then tested various methods of locomotion, settling on loping as the most economical. He also collected soil samples, left a seismic experiment package, and then set up a retro-reflector so that laser beams could be bounced off the Moon's surface to determine its exact distance from Earth.

Armstrong helped plant the Stars and Stripes and then spoke with Richard Nixon. He also took several photographs of the lunar module and the surrounding craters, as well as collecting rock samples. After two and a half hours outside the landing module, he and Aldrin then returned to the *Eagle* with their samples. Once safely inside, they pressurized the cabin and settled down to rest. While

moving in the tiny cabin, however, Aldrin broke the circuit breaker that armed the main engine. He eventually discovered that the tip of a pen could activate the switch.

The *Eagle* then lifted off from the Moon to rendezvous with Collins in *Columbia*. The ascent stage was jettisoned whereupon its orbit gradually disintegrated until it crashed into the Moon several months later. On July 24th the command module re-entered Earth's atmosphere and splashed down in the Pacific Ocean 1,400 miles from Wake Island. The module was recovered by the crew of the USS *Hornet*, although the astronauts then spent three weeks in quarantine in case they'd brought back any pathogens from the Moon.

On August 10th 1969 they were allowed out of confinement, and three days later they were given ticker-tape parades in New York, Chicago and Los Angeles. They then embarked on a world tour to celebrate perhaps the greatest technological achievement in the history of mankind. It will only be surpassed when people first walk on the surface of Mars.

Michael Collins went on to become director of the National Air and Space

Above:
Armstrong, Collins and Aldrin a few months before the launch of Apollo 11

Museum. He also became undersecretary of the Smithsonian Institution and vide-president of LTV Aerospace. He and wife Pat spend their time between Florida and North Carolina.

Buzz Aldrin left NASA to become commandant of Edwards AFB but he retired from active service in 1972.

He battled depression and alcoholism while continuing to promote space exploration. Having recovered from these illnesses, Aldrin expressed his support for a mission to Mars and he continues to live a public life.

Neil Armstrong only spent another year with the space administration

before taking a teaching position at the University of Cincinnati. He resigned in 1979 to serve on the board of directors for a number of high-profile companies, although by then he had largely withdrawn from public life because he was tired of the attention and wished to live as private a life as possible. He died following heart surgery in August 2012. Although he was almost deified as an all-American hero, he was a courageous and humble man who had served his country proudly and with great distinction. The achievements of all three are rightly recognised as among the most significant in human history.

Dame Nellie Bly

Nellie Bly was the pen name of American journalist Elizabeth Cochran. She was born in the suburbs of Pittsburgh in May 1864 to Michael, a labourer, and Mary Jane. Her father impressed on her the value of hard work and he eventually bought the local mill. Elizabeth went to boarding school but only lasted a term before her parents ran out of money.

In 1880 the family moved into central Pittsburgh. Elizabeth then read a sexist article in a local newspaper so she penned a fiery reply and sent it to the editor, George Madden. He was so impressed with her that he offered her a job with the paper. Female journalists usually chose pen names so Elizabeth chose Nellie Bly. She initially wrote investigative pieces highlighting the plight of working women but she then moved into fashion, society and gardening.

Disillusioned with the direction the paper was taking, she asked to be posted to Mexico to serve as its foreign correspondent while still only 21. Madden accepted but Bly was forced to leave the country after criticising dictator Porfirio Díaz. She then moved to New York and took an undercover assignment in a mental hospital for Joseph Pulitzer's *New York World*.

Having convinced doctors she was insane, she was sent to Blackwell Island Asylum. Conditions were appalling: the food was often rotten and inedible, the water was dirty, human waste was everywhere, and the seriously ill patients were roped together and beaten regularly.

After 10 days of intolerable treatment that would send most people insane, the newspaper demanded that she be released. Her scathing report brought her to the attention of the public and convinced the government to increase funding into diagnosis and treatment of the mentally ill.

In 1888, Bly approached her editor with an idea for recreating the journey from *Around the World in Eighty Days*. He agreed as long as she sent regular reports via the new telegraph network. A year later, on November 14th, Bly boarded the Hamburg-America steamer *Augusta Victoria* with precious few clothes or belongings and little money and began her epic trip. Rival paper *Cosmopolitan* dispatched Elizabeth Bisland to beat both Bly and Phileas Fogg, so interest in what was now clearly a race increased dramatically (Bisland travelled west while Bly went east).

Nellie Bly arrived in England before heading to France to meet Jules Verne in Amiens. She then passed through the Suez Canal before stopping in first the Middle East and then Ceylon (now Sri Lanka). Having also visited Singapore, a leper colony in China,

Hong Kong and Japan – travelling predominantly by antiquated railway and tramp steamer – she headed across the Pacific aboard White Star's *Oceanic*.

Bad weather slowed her crossing and she arrived in San Francisco two days behind schedule so Pulitzer helped her out by chartering a train to bring her back to New York. She arrived in Hoboken after her largely unaccompanied circumnavigation of the world on January 25th 1890. Her time of 72 days 6 hours and 11 minutes meant she beat Bisland by four days, although George Francis Train lowered her mark by five days a few months later.

In later life she married manufacturing millionaire Robert Seaman who was 40 years her senior. When he died in 1904 she became one of the country's leading industrialists and a part-time inventor (garbage cans that stacked and a new type of milk container), although her employees embezzled much of her estate and forced her into bankruptcy. She continued writing prolifically before dying of pneumonia in New York in 1922.

Sir Richard Burton

Sir Richard Burton was born in Devon in March 1821 to Lieutenant-Colonel Joseph Burton, an army officer of Anglo-Irish descent, and Martha Baker, a wealthy heiress from Hertfordshire. The family travelled widely throughout Europe during his youth so Burton was home taught by tutors, although he was also educated in Richmond. By then he spoke French, Italian and Latin, as well as several dialects.

He enrolled at Oxford and continued studying languages, although he also learnt falconry and fencing. He apparently challenged a fellow student to a duel after he mocked Burton's moustache and he was then expelled from Trinity College after violating the rules by going to a steeplechase.

Burton promptly enlisted in the army of the East India Company in the hope of fighting in the Afghan War but he was posted to Gujarat instead. He spent his downtime learning Indian dialects and customs to the point where he'd almost gone native, although he was also known as a demonic fighter who had fought more enemies in hand-to-hand combat than any man alive.

In 1849 he returned to Europe on sick leave and visited the fencing school in Boulogne, where he met a young aristocratic woman, Isabel Arundell, who would later become his wife. He had an insatiable appetite for adventure, however, so he asked for permission to leave the army and make a pilgrimage to Mecca (a Hajj). Made in 1853, it was this journey that made him famous. He had to adopt various disguises and was required to master Islamic traditions and etiquette to complete the journey, and he also had

to fight off bandits in the desert.

His next expedition to Somalia and the African interior took him to Harar in Ethiopia (he was the first European to enter the city), where he was entertained by the Emir for 10 days. Burton almost died of thirst on the return leg but found water just in time. He immediately set about organising another trek but 200 Somali warriors attacked his party before they left camp. Burton was struck in the face with a javelin that pierced both cheeks, although he eventually managed to escape.

Having fought briefly in the Crimea, Burton convinced the Royal Geographic Society to fund another expedition to find Africa's inland sea, which had been documented by Arab traders. He set off from Zanzibar in June 1857 and headed west in search of the mythical lakes with the help of Omani Arabs. Although he and his team contracted all kinds of tropical maladies, Burton arrived at Lake Tanganyika in February 1858. His surveying equipment was largely ruined by then so Burton returned to Zanzibar. His travelling companion, John Speke, despite being blinded and deafened by disease, remained behind and found Lake Victoria, which he claimed must be the source of the Nile.

Burton kept detailed notes on all of his travels and these proved invaluable for the later expeditions of Stanley and Livingstone, amongst others. However, he and Speke soon fell out over their claims, their impact on the African people, and the debts racked up by their travels. The two men then made every effort to undermine the other's reputation.

Burton and Isabel married in 1861 but he spent the next four years mapping the coast of West Africa and travelling up the River Congo to beyond the Yellala Falls. When he was posted to Brazil in 1865, Burton explored the country's central highlands. He was then made consul in Damascus, although his abrasive style and unconventional personality led to tension with the Jewish, Christian and Muslim population. Indeed his irascible nature is often cited as the reason why he wasn't promoted in either the army or the diplomatic service.

Burton was a prolific writer about his adventures, although most of his books were considered too risqué as they usually detailed the sexual practices of the peoples he encountered. He co-founded the Anthropological Society of London in 1863 and was knighted by Queen Victoria in 1886. By then he was reportedly fluent in 40 languages and dialects.

He died in Trieste in 1890 but was buried in a tomb designed by Isabel in Mortlake, London. Somewhat controversially, she burned most of Burton's papers after his death, denying future generations access to his wealth of knowledge and experiences in the Middle East, Africa and South America.

Christopher Columbus

Christopher Columbus was born in October 1451 in Genoa to Domenico Colombo, a middle-class wool weaver, and Susanna Fontanarossa. He had three brothers and a sister. His name is an Anglicisation of the Latin Christophorus Columbus, although he is also known as Cristoforo Colombo (Italian) and Cristóbal Colón (Spanish).

Columbus claims to have first gone to sea in 1461 and, by 1470, he had been hired by the Genoese to help conquer Naples. Three years later he became a businessman for the ruling Genoese families and was often required to accompany cargoes throughout Northern Europe, including to Britain, Ireland and Iceland. It's possible that during these trips he heard tales of Erik the Red and Leif Erikson, the latter of whom is now credited with discovering North America.

Columbus then moved to Lisbon and married Filipa Moniz Perestrelo, daughter of the governor of Porto Santo. His son Diego was born in 1479 but Columbus was trading along the African coast for much of his early childhood. Filipa either died or was abandoned by Columbus in 1485. Two years later he was living with a mistress, Beatriz de Arana, in Castile.

Europeans had always been granted safe passage along the Silk Road to the Far East but, with the fall of Constantinople to the Turks in 1453, the overland route to Asia became a dangerous proposition. Explorers and traders decided to pioneer a route east to the Spice Islands by rounding the Cape of Good Hope in South Africa. In 1470 the astronomer Paolo Toscanelli suggested that the islands of Southeast Asia might also be reached by sailing west

across the Atlantic.

As it was widely known that the Earth was roughly spherical, Columbus, an experienced mariner, knew that sailing west would eventually lead to the Indies. However, he underestimated the size of the planet, overestimated the size of the Eurasian landmass, and miscalculated the distance between the inhabited islands to the east of China (all of which was at odds with conventional scientific and nautical wisdom). He eventually concluded that the distance from the Canary Islands to Japan was only around 2,300 miles, whereas it's actually 12,200 miles, far further than a ship could travel without having to stop for fresh food and water.

While most navigators knew the westward journey was unfeasible, Columbus promised to open a lucrative

Above: A painting depicting Columbus's landing in the New World

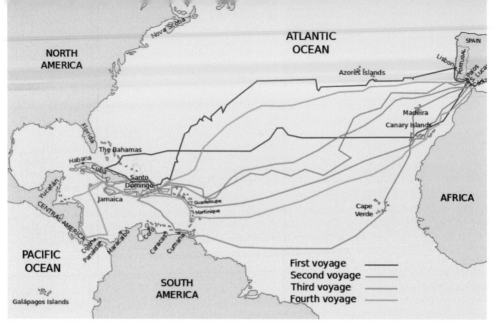

Above: *The voyages of Christopher Columbus*

trade route. He submitted proposals for his journey to King John II of Portugal in 1485 but was rejected. Three years later he was dismissed again because the route around the southern tip of Africa had now been pioneered. He eventually managed to convince King Ferdinand and Queen Isabella of Castile to finance the voyage.

In August 1492 Columbus's expedition left Palos de la Frontera in three ships: the Niña, the Pinta and the Santa María. He restocked in the Canary Islands and then spent five weeks crossing the Atlantic before landing (most likely on San Salvador Island in the Bahamas) on October 12th. The indigenous people were largely peaceful but vulnerable due to their primitive technology. Columbus took several prisoners and then continued exploring Cuba, although he also left men behind to help convert the natives to Christianity. He returned in triumph to Lisbon in March 1493, and word of his discovery of a new world spread rapidly throughout Europe.

Later in the year he made a second voyage with 17 ships and more than 1,000 men. His mission was primarily one of peaceful colonisation and conversion, although many of his crew captured female prisoners to take as wives. The expedition eventually discovered Dominica, Guadeloupe, Montserrat, Antigua, Saint Kitts & Nevis, Puerto Rico, the Antilles and Virgin islands, amongst many others. He reached Jamaica in May before returning to Hispaniola and then heading east to Spain.

His third voyage, which saw him reach Trinidad and then South America, ended in humiliation as the colonists on Hispaniola rebelled against his rule and had him sent back to Spain in irons. Although Columbus was stripped of his governorship, he was allowed to return to the New World a fourth time in 1502. He explored the Central American coast from Honduras to Panama but was then stranded in Jamaica for a year when his ships were damaged by storms. He finally arrived back in Spain in November 1504.

Although his achievements as a navigator and explorer are rightly applauded, Columbus's methods of governing the natives are not. He ruled with an iron fist and regularly had people mutilated, dismembered and executed for opposing him. Thousands were eventually slaughtered during his seven-

Above:
Columbus's tomb
in Seville

year tenure over the Bahamas.

He suffered all manner of ailments during later life and died aged around 54 in Valladolid, Spain, in May 1506. Although it was believed that he had discovered the Americas, both the indigenous people and the Vikings got there first. Columbus, however, returned to Europe with news from the continent, as well as making several epic voyages of discovery. And for that his place in the history of exploration is secure.

Captain James Cook

Captain James Cook was born to James and Grace in October 1728 in Yorkshire. When he was eight the family moved to Great Ayton and he went to the local school before working for his father on Airey Holme Farm. After two years he moved to Whitby and was introduced to the Walker family who were local ship owners in the coal trade. Cook signed up aboard their collier *Freelove* as an apprentice. While plying the coal route between London and Tyneside, he taught himself the skills he would need to command his own ship in the future, notably trigonometry and celestial navigation.

Cook then worked on trading ships in the Baltics and soon progressed to the rank of mate in the merchant navy. To advance his career, he then volunteered for the Royal Navy as it was preparing for the Seven Years' War. He served aboard HMS *Eagle* from 1755 and briefly took command of a cutter the following year. In 1757 he passed his master's exams and joined HMS *Solebay*.

Cook was a superb surveyor and cartographer and his maps were used extensively during the war in what would become Canadian waters. He then mapped the Saint Lawrence River, the coast of Newfoundland, the Burin Peninsula and Cape Ray. Having also employed local pilots to list rocks and other hazards, he submitted his maps to the admiralty and the Royal Society (they would be used well into the 20th century).

In 1766 the Royal Society commissioned him to observe the transit of Venus from the Pacific

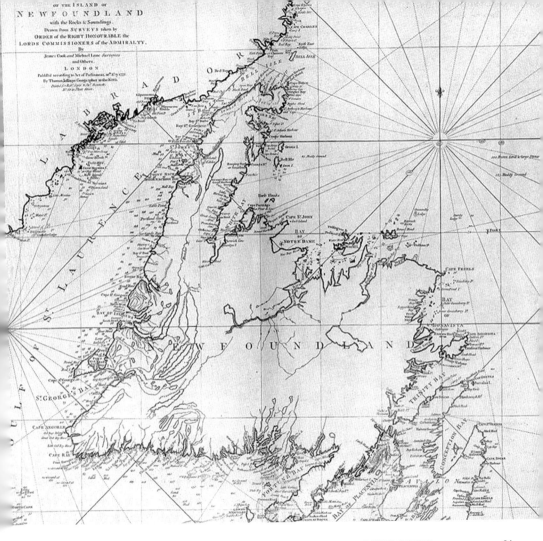

Ocean. He was immediately promoted to lieutenant and given command of the *Endeavour*. The ship sailed in 1768, rounding Cape Horn at the tip of South America and arriving in Tahiti the following year. The crew recorded the celestial transit before mapping the entire coast of New Zealand. They then sailed west and became the first Europeans to land on the east coast of Australia (at Botany Bay). Cook also became the first person to make contact with the indigenous aboriginal people.

Endeavour then sailed north along the Great Barrier Reef, through the Torres Strait to Possession Island and then west to Jakarta. Although he lost several crewmen along the way, the ship rounded the Cape of Good Hope, stopped briefly on Saint Helena in 1771 and then returned to England.

Cook's journals made him a national hero and he was promoted to commander before being recruited by the Royal Society – who believed a larger continent lay to the south of the one documented by Cook – for a second voyage of discovery. HMS *Resolution* and HMS *Adventure* sailed south and crossed the Antarctic Circle in January 1773 but the ships then became separated in fog. *Adventure* headed back to England while Cook continued exploring the Antarctic, although he just missed the continental landmass. On his return to New Zealand he visited the Friendly Islands, Easter Island and Vanuatu, amongst others. He claimed South Georgia for the crown on his way home and submitted maps of such beauty and accuracy that they were still being used in 1950 (John Harrison's marine chronometer allowed him to calculate longitude much more accurately than previous sailors).

Cook was promoted to post–captain and was then retired from the navy, although he accepted only if he could return to active duty for a suitable assignment. In 1776, he took command of *Resolution* once more and headed for the Pacific to try to find the fabled Northwest Passage that was rumoured to lead back into the Atlantic. In January 1778 he became the first European to visit Hawaii, and he then mapped most of the west coast of North America – from California to Alaska – in a single visit.

Having failed to navigate the Bering Strait, Cook returned to Hawaii, where he was greeted as a kind of deity.

However, shortly after leaving the islands, his ship's mast broke so he made repairs in Kealakekua Bay. The locals here were not as friendly and they stole one of his cutters. Cook retaliated by marching through the village to kidnap the King of Hawaii, Kalani'ōpu'u. At first, the king agreed to go willingly but, when the villagers saw what was happening, they massed on the shore and clubbed Cook over the head. He and several marines were then stabbed to death. Cook was still revered by the islanders, however, so he was given a chief's funeral before some of his bones were returned to his crew for a formal burial at sea. His ships returned to England in 1780.

Cook's legacy is almost incalculable: he charted Hawaii, New Zealand, many more of the Pacific Islands, eastern Australia and the west and east coasts of North America. He theorised that there were links – later proven – between all the peoples of the Pacific Basin, and he was the first European contact for thousands of islanders. His contributions to astronomy, botany, science and navigation are without equal and he remains one of the greatest explorers and ambassadors of all time.

Amelia Earhart

Amelia Earhart was born in Kansas in July 1897 to Edwin, a lawyer, and Amy. She and her sister, Grace, were allowed the freedom of the neighbourhood and they soon developed a spirit of adventure. Earhart hunted rats, collected flora and fauna, and even built a ramp for a homemade sled, although her first flight ended painfully. The family moved to Des Moines in Iowa in 1907 and Earhart soon saw her first aircraft at the state fair, although she was uninterested in the rickety biplane and was much happier on the merry-go-round.

She was taught at home initially but then went to public school. Soon afterwards it became apparent that her father was an alcoholic and, when her grandmother died suddenly, the family house was auctioned and her childhood came to an abrupt end. She eventually graduated from Hyde Park High School in 1916 and promptly trained as a nurse to care for wounded soldiers returning from the battlefields of Europe.

She was taken seriously ill during the Spanish Flu epidemic in 1918 and spent nearly a year recovering. She then visited an airfield in Long Beach where future air racer Frank Hawks gave her a 10-minute ride. It was the moment Earhart's life changed: she was now determined to become a pilot herself. She saved every penny she earned and took her first flight in a Curtiss JN-4 in January 1921 with instructor Anita Snook.

Six months later, she bought her first plane, which she nicknamed 'The Canary'. In October the following year she took the little biplane to 14,000 feet and set a new world altitude record for

women. In May 1923 she became only the 16th woman to be issued with a pilot's licence.

The family then fell on hard times, however, so Earhart bought a car and drove her recently divorced mother from California to Boston via Calgary. Although she then took a number of odd jobs, she maintained her interest in flying and promoted aviation in local newspaper columns. This brought her to the attention of publicist George Putnam,

who was co-sponsoring a trans-Atlantic flight, and he suggested she become the first woman to fly to Europe. Although she didn't take the controls (the flying was left to pilot Wilmer Stultz), she received a rousing welcome in England in June 1928, and an even greater reception on her return home, where President Calvin Coolidge invited her to the White House.

Having embarked on a lecture tour, Putnam suggested he promote her in a marketing campaign and she was soon something of a celebrity. The subsequent endorsements helped finance her flying career, and she and Charles Lindbergh used their newfound status to promote commercial air travel. A passenger service between New York and Washington, DC soon developed into TWA. Another of her local air operations then morphed into Northeast Airlines.

In August 1928 she became the first woman to fly solo across North America and back, and the following year she entered several air races. Having married Putnam in 1931, she then flew solo non-stop across the Atlantic to Ireland in a Lockheed Vega, for which she was extensively decorated. In 1935 she became the first person to fly solo from Hawaii to California, and she then set another seven speed and distance records, after which she set her sights on an equatorial circumnavigation of the globe.

She bought and modified a Lockheed Electra, and then chose Fred Noonan as chief navigator as he was vastly experienced with marine and celestial navigation. Secondary navigator Henry Manning and Earhart's instructor Paul Mantz also made the first leg of the trip from Oakland to Honolulu. The aircraft was then grounded for three days to repair minor problems with the propellers' pitch mechanisms. When resuming the flight, Earhart's Electra ground-looped on take-off and crashed. Mantz cited pilot error as the cause, although witnesses said they thought a tyre had burst, and Earhart believed the landing gear had collapsed. The crew survived but the aircraft was so badly damaged that it had to be shipped back to Burbank for repairs.

Earhart and Putnam managed to fund a second attempt in May 1937, only this time she would fly east with only Noonan for company. The flight was largely uneventful and they travelled via South America, Africa, India and Southeast Asia before landing in New Guinea in late June. The last 7,000 miles from Lae to mainland North America would have to be flown via Howland Island and then Honolulu.

Earhart and Noonan left Lae late at night on the 2,500-mile flight to Howland Island and they initially made good progress. However, a series of misunderstandings and possible unfamiliarity with their radio and navigational equipment meant they were low on fuel as they approached the tiny sliver of land in the Pacific. The coastguard cutter *Itasca* was supposed to guide the Electra in but they had difficultly communicating with Earhart and Noonan because the pilots didn't appear to be able to hear their transmissions. In the early hours of the morning, however, the crew on the *Itasca* picked up Earhart's radio messages with complete clarity, which meant the aircraft must have been in the immediate area.

Earhart dropped to 1,000 feet to search for the island but still didn't see it or the cutter. As she couldn't hear them, the crew of the *Itasca* sent replies in Morse Code that were acknowledged by Earhart and Noonan, although they were unable to take a bearing on the transmissions to follow them in. Her last known message at 8.43am said she was flying along a sun line north and south in the hope of spotting the island through the scattered

Opposite: *Earhart and her beloved Vega*

Right: *Amelia Earhart and the Lockheed Electra flown by her and Fred Noonan*

cloud. The *Itasca* generated smoke for several hours but Earhart and Noonan didn't see the signal and disappeared completely. Several indistinct radio transmissions were heard for the next few days but, despite an intensive search operation, Earhart and Noonan's Electra was never seen again.

Many theories have been suggested – from ditching at sea to being captured and executed by the Japanese because she was spying for the US – but the most likely scenario is that, having failed to spot Howland, Earhart continued southeast until she and Noonan saw Nikumaroro (Gardner Island), whereupon they tried to land on the island's exposed reef. It's possible that they survived on the island for several days but without food and water they would soon have succumbed to starvation and/or exposure. Enormous carnivorous coconut crabs populate the lagoon so their remains may well have been eaten.

Gerald Gallagher found a skeleton on the island in 1940. Having been taken to Fiji, British authorities claimed it was of a local man but recent analysis of their findings (the bones were misplaced by the Fijians years ago so this analysis is based on the original British report) suggests that

the bones belonged to a tall white female of European descent.

The bones were found with a sextant box so a research expedition to the island was organised in 2007. The team found a campsite, improvised tools, an aluminium panel that could have come from the aircraft, a piece of Plexiglas identical to that used in the Electra's windows, the remains of a woman's compact beauty case containing 1930s-era skincare products, and part of a shoe resembling the make worn by Earhart.

A later expedition found bronze bearings and a zipper that could have come from a flight suit. In 2013, the same team discovered wreckage near the reef that could be the Electra (photos taken just before the war appear to show the remains of the Electra's landing gear still

visible on the reef). When some of the radio transmissions from immediately after the aircraft's disappearance were re-examined, one contained a reference to the ship SS *Norwich City* (the wrecked freighter lies just off the island having run aground on the reef in 1929). As the island was uninhabited at the time, only Noonan or Earhart would have mentioned the ship in the hope that it

would lead rescuers to them.

Whatever her fate, Amelia Earhart inspired thousands of women to pursue a career in aviation. Her bashful charisma, determination and courage enabled her to break countless records, and her exploits ensured she achieved lasting fame. She has been honoured with hundreds of tributes and memorials, and she remains an icon of popular culture.

Leif Erikson

Leif Erikson was born to Erik the Red and Thjodhild in Iceland in the late 10th century. His grandfather, Thorvaldr Ásvaldsson, was Norwegian but he was banished from his homeland for manslaughter. Erik the Red was then banished from Iceland, so he established a settlement in Greenland in 986 AD.

While Leif was in his late teens or early 20s he travelled from Greenland to Norway and was seconded into King Olaf Tryggvason's private army. Having converted to Christianity, Olaf then tasked him with bringing religion to Greenland. While making the crossing to Greenland, Erikson's ship was blown off course and he eventually sighted an unfamiliar coastline. He hadn't expected to reach land, especially a rich and fertile place with wheat fields and grapevines, but he stepped ashore and then rescued two shipwrecked mariners. Having returned to Greenland, he converted the small population to Christianity.

While translations of the early written sagas suggest that although Erikson did reach North America – the Vikings called it Vinland – he might not have been the first European to visit the New World. That distinction goes to Bjarni Herjólfsson, a merchant who also strayed off course and sighted Vinland in 986. Accounts of his voyage in later years suggest he didn't make landfall but returned instead to Greenland. When Erikson heard about the new lands to the west, he bought Herjólfsson's boat and retraced his voyage.

It's likely that Erikson first made land on Baffin Island before heading further south to Labrador. After two more days at sea, he landed in a place teeming

with salmon. He eventually established a settlement at L'Anse aux Meadows in Newfoundland. While half of his team wintered at the settlement, the other half explored the region and found it to be rich with vines and timber, which they then transported back to Greenland.

Erikson was considered wise and thoughtful, and his exploits convinced other Norse people to make the journey west. His son, Thorvald, was apparently the first European to make contact with the indigenous people of North America but the two camps were hostile to one another and permanent settlements on the mainland were abandoned (expeditions for timber did continue for centuries). No mention of Erikson can be found in the literature after 1019, and by 1025 his son Thorkell had inherited his chieftaincy, so it's likely he died in the intervening years.

Above: *A painting showing Leif Erikson discovering North America*

Sir Ranulph Fiennes

Sir Ranulph Fiennes was born in Windsor in March 1944. His father had just been killed in action commanding the Royal Scots Greys, so Fiennes inherited his baronetcy at birth (he is a distant cousin of the royal family). His mother moved to South Africa after the war so Fiennes went to Western Province Prep School in Cape Town. He then returned to the UK and went to Eton before joining the British Army.

Fiennes served in his father's regiment and was then seconded to the demolitions outfit of the Special Air Service where he became the youngest captain in the army. After trying to blow up a dam built by 20th Century Fox for the film *Doctor Dolittle* as a practical joke, he went on the run but was eventually captured and discharged from the SAS. He spent another two years as part of the Sultan of Oman's army and saw extensive service in the Dhofar Rebellion, for which he was decorated with the Sultan's Bravery Medal.

Having left the military, Fiennes auditioned unsuccessfully for the part of James Bond and then embarked on a number of adventures, including leading a hovercraft expedition up the White Nile in 1969. Between 1979 and 1982 he and two former SAS colleagues, Oliver Shepard and Charles Burton, completed a circumnavigation of the globe via its polar axis using surface transport only. It remains the only such trip ever undertaken.

Leaving Greenwich in 1979, they headed south and reached the Antarctic pole on December 17th 1980. It took them another 14 months to reach the

North Pole and they arrived back in London in August 1982. The trip also involved completing the infamous Northwest Passage in an 18-foot Boston Whaler, which took 36 days and was the first west to east open-boat transit. He returned to the South Pole in 1993 with Doctor Mike Stroud, the pair making the first unsupported crossing of the continent.

He had to abandon solo trips to the poles in 1996 (south) and 2000 (north) due to kidney stones and sled failure respectively, and he also lost the tips of several fingers to frostbite in the latter attempt (he amputated the necrotic flesh himself in his garden shed).

He didn't let a heart attack in 2003 slow him down either. Only four months after leaving hospital he and Stroud ran seven marathons on seven continents in seven days. He then climbed the treacherous North Face of the Eiger before becoming the oldest Briton to summit Mount Everest. In so doing, he became the only person in history to cross both polar ice caps and stand on top of the world.

In 2013 he was forced to abandon the first attempt to cross Antarctica in winter because of extreme frostbite. Despite this, his expeditions have raised £15 million

for various causes. He was awarded the Polar Medal in 1986, an OBE in 1993 and the Royal Geographic Society's Founder's Medal in 2012. *The Guinness Book of Records* still lists him as the greatest living explorer.

Above: *Sir Ranulph Fiennes in the shadow of Everest*

Sir John Franklin

Sir John Franklin was born to Willingham and Hannah in Lincolnshire in 1786. Having attended King Edward VI Grammar School he announced his intention to pursue a career at sea. He signed up with a merchant ship at the age of 14 but soon joined the navy aboard HMS *Polyphemus*.

Franklin then found himself serving alongside Horatio Nelson at the Battle of Copenhagen in 1801 and at Trafalgar four years later, and he also fought against the United States at the Battle of New Orleans in 1815.

In 1819 Franklin was asked by the Royal Navy to navigate the Coppermine River in Canada in the hope that the expedition would discover the fabled Northwest Passage. The trip suffered from poor planning and a reliance on local people but the party finally reached Cumberland House, a log cabin on the trading route, where they spent a particularly harsh winter. Indeed the native Indians reported that some tribes were resorting to cannibalism to survive.

In January the team set out again but they suffered terribly from the cold, a lack of supplies and increasing hostility from the locals. The party mutinied at the end of the summer, with some having to be sent back south to their base at Fort Enterprise. The following spring, Franklin continued his troublesome journey down the Coppermine River but they didn't reach the Arctic Ocean until July 1821. He somehow managed to map 500 miles of coastline from three damaged canoes before taking the decision to return to the river overland.

Another severe winter saw their rations exhausted so the party was reduced to foraging for rotten carcasses, eaten lichen and even boiling their spare boots to chew on the leather. They finally reached the Coppermine in September but their canoes were useless and it took them days to build another, by which time the party had all but disintegrated.

Having crossed the river and begun the march back to Fort Enterprise, Franklin's men began to succumb to starvation and exhaustion, and several of the party had to be left to make their own way back to the fort. He and five men finally staggered into Fort Enterprise having survived on tea and leather for four weeks, but the camp hadn't been resupplied in their absence. A few days later, one of the men who had been left for dead, Michel Terohaute, then stumbled into the fort with a supply of meat. The men gorged themselves for several

days until it became evident that Terohaute had murdered some of the stragglers for food. The aggressive and increasingly erratic Terohaute then shot expedition member Robert Hood, and it wasn't until three days later that John Richardson finally managed to disarm and shoot him. The party was eventually rescued by Akaitcho, a local Indian, in November 1821.

The expedition had been a disaster. Despite covering 5,500 miles, Franklin only mapped 500 miles of coastline and managed to lose 11 of his 19 men. However, he managed to survive the accusations of cannibalism with his reputation intact and, having been promoted and elected a Fellow of the Royal Society, he was sent on a second expedition to the Arctic in 1825.

With much better organisation, the trip was a great success and Franklin reached Great Slave Lake before charting 1,000 miles of the MacKenzie River to its mouth. Having returned safely to the UK, he then spent four years as Lieutenant-Governor of Van Diemen's Land (Tasmania). The British then removed him from his post and charged him with completing his mission to navigate the Northwest Passage.

Although the two ships earmarked for the expedition – HMS *Erebus* and HMS *Terror* – were well-suited and stocked, the cans of food and fresh-water supply were probably contaminated with lead from poor soldering and period pipe-work respectively. The ships were last seen by the whaler *Prince of Wales* when moored to an iceberg in Lancaster Sound. It's likely that they then became trapped in ice off King William Island (a note found on the island announced that Franklin had died there in June 1847).

As they had supplies for three years, a search party wasn't sent until later that year, but by 1850 the large reward and Franklin's fame meant that more ships had joined the hunt. On the east coast of Beechey Island, several graves were found but it wasn't until 1854 that Scotsman John Rae learned what had happened from the Inuit. They claimed that when the ships became icebound, the crews had tried to reach safety on foot before eventually turning on each other. Later studies of the bones revealed that the men had died from a combination of pneumonia, tuberculosis, lead poisoning, scurvy, botulism and, as had long been suspected, cannibalism.

Vasco da Gama

Vasco da Gama was born between 1460 and 1469 in Sines, Portugal. His father, Estêvão, was a knight to Ferdinand, Duke of Viseu, and then governor of Sines, while his mother, Isabel Sodré, was from a well-connected English family. Little can be found about Vasco's youth in the historical record but it's likely he studied maths and navigation, possibly under the astronomer Abraham Zacuto.

Da Gama then joined his father in the Order of Santiago under Prince John (who would later accede to the Portuguese throne). As a man who moved in royal circles, Da Gama was on hand to be recruited for a raid on French ships in the Algarve in 1492. His mission was successful so five years later he was given command of a fleet of four ships with the aim of establishing a trade route around the Cape of Good Hope and into the Indian Ocean.

Da Gama left Lisbon in July 1497 and made landfall along the west coast of Africa after stopping at the traditional ports of Tenerife and the Cape Verde Islands. Having crossed the equator, the ships spent three months in the mid-Atlantic, covering 6,000 miles, comfortably the longest journey yet made out of sight of land. At the end of the year, the ships rounded the cape before exploring much of the east coast of Africa, a continent that Da Gama realised stretched thousands of miles to the northeast. He visited Mozambique, Mombasa and Malindi, whereupon they discovered evidence of the locals trading with the subcontinent to the east.

In April 1498, Da Gama's ships left Malindi with a local pilot and sailed for

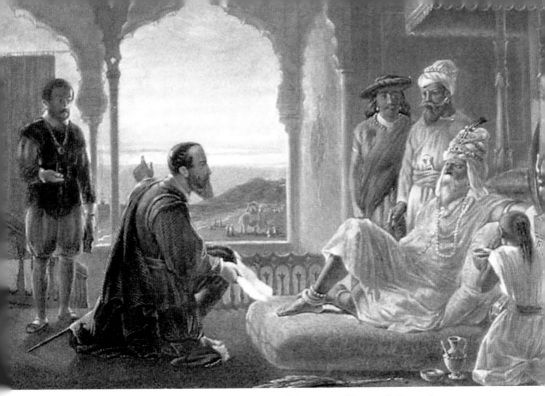

Above: *A steel engraving depicting Da Gama's meeting with Zamorin in May 1498*

southwest India. The fleet landed at Kappadu in late May and King Zamorin of Calicut welcomed them with a 3,000-strong procession. Da Gama's gifts of cloaks, hats, sugar, oil and honey weren't as well-received however, and Zamorin began to suspect that the lack of precious metals in his cargo meant that Da Gama must be a pirate rather than a special envoy of the King of Portugal. Zamorin eventually insisted that he pay customs duty in gold so Da Gama kidnapped 20 locals and escaped with cargo worth many times the cost of his journey.

Da Gama's return trip across the Indian Ocean was against the wind and it took four months instead of the three weeks on the outbound leg. They finally

Above: A painting showing Vasco da Gama leaving Portugal

sighted land at Mogadishu in Somalia but they didn't dock and sailed back down the African coast to Malindi. It had been a costly crossing in human terms and Da Gama no longer had enough crew for all three ships. The *São Rafael* was scuttled leaving the *São Gabriel* and the *Berrio* to complete the return journey.

When Da Gama's brother, Paulo, fell ill in the Cape Verde islands, Vasco remained with him while the ships returned to Lisbon. Paulo eventually died in the Azores so Da Gama joined a caravel returning to Lisbon and only arrived in August 1499. He was given a hero's welcome and was immediately decorated by Manuel I for opening a direct sea route to Asia and returning with spices worth a small fortune, although he had failed his principal mission to negotiate a trade agreement with the King of Calicut.

In 1500 Pedro Cabral led a fleet to Calicut to try once more to establish a trade treaty with Zamorin but local Arab merchants killed 70 of Cabral's men, for which he blamed Zamorin. Portugal thus declared war on Calicut. Da Gama was sent to intervene with a fleet of 15 ships and 800 men. His cousin then followed in a second wave that included two of Da Gama's uncles and his brothers-in-law.

Da Gama negotiated a settlement with the port of Sofala in East Africa and then set about capturing any Arab ship in the Indian Ocean. He then burned all the passengers and crew aboard a pilgrim ship even though they begged for mercy and could have bought their way out of trouble with a fabulous haul of gold and jewels. Then, when Zamorin refused

to expel all Muslims from Calicut, Da Gama's ships pounded the unfortified city for two days and his men mutilated the crews of ships captured entering the port. Zamorin retaliated by sending his fleet into battle, although Da Gama's ships were far superior and sank most of them in the harbour.

This appalling brutality meant he was overlooked for the role of governor and viceroy of Portuguese India. He was shunned by King Manuel for the next two decades until he threatened to defect to the crown of Castile (as Magellan had). Manuel reinstated him with a feudal title and, upon the king's death in 1521, Da Gama emerged from the political wilderness as an advisor to his successor, John III.

John sent Da Gama east to India as its new viceroy in April 1524 with a fleet of 14 ships. Five were lost en route but Da Gama eventually arrived in September and replaced most of the government officials with his own men. He contracted malaria immediately, however, and died in Cochin on Christmas Eve. His body was buried but his remains were eventually returned to Portugal in 1539.

Zheng He

Zheng He was born into a Muslim family of Hui people in Yunnan, China, in 1371. His Persian forefathers served in the administration of the Mongol Empire and many were known as Hajji, which meant they had made the pilgrimage to Mecca either by land or sea. Hearing of their stories in his youth, Zheng He quickly developed a fascination with the ocean and was devoted to Tianfei, the goddess of seafarers.

In late 1381, a Ming Dynasty army conquered Yunnan and Zheng He's father was a victim of the campaign. Zheng He was captured, castrated (as was the custom for many prisoners of war), and put to work under Zhu Di, Prince of Yan, in Beiping (which would become Peking and then Beijing). In his teens, Zheng He was drafted into the army and

fought against the Mongols, earning the gratitude and then the respect of Zhu Di.

Zhu Di eventually became Yongle Emperor (the third emperor of the Ming Dynasty) but he was overlooked in favour of his nephew for the emperorship of Jianwen. When the two families went to war in 1399, Zheng He commanded Zhu Di's forces against the imperial army. In 1402, Zheng He defeated imperial forces and marched into Nanjing, whereupon Zhu Di promoted him to Grand Director of the Palace Servants as well as Chief Envoy.

In 1405 the Ming government sponsored several naval expeditions to expand Chinese knowledge of the world to the west into the Indian Ocean basin. Zheng He was promoted to admiral and given command of an enormous fleet of 317 ships – some as large as 400 feet

according to historians – and 28,000 men. During these voyages of discovery, the fleet sailed to Champa, Java, Brunei, Thailand, Malaysia, Sri Lanka, India, Arabia, Hormuz and East Africa and traded successfully with the local people, particularly in Arabia and Africa. The trade routes may have been mapped from the Han Dynasty around 1,000 years earlier, and there were already Chinese settlers in Malacca (in the Malayan Peninsula), but the size of the fleet hinted that the missions were to establish permanent trading posts throughout the Indian Ocean as well as mapping new shipping routes.

The army at his disposal was largely for show and Zheng He usually achieved his goals through peaceful diplomacy, although he did hunt down pirates and wasn't afraid to wage land wars against inhospitable tribes in Africa and unfriendly officials in Arabia.

Zheng He returned home from his last voyage in 1433 having visited more than 30 foreign kingdoms and mapped vast areas of the subcontinent and Africa. There are varying accounts of his death but he either died the same year or two years later while defending Nanjing from invaders. Although his achievements were played down by imperial officials following his death, his maritime and navigational legacy is almost without equal.

Above: *A map depicting the voyages of Zheng He*

Thor Heyerdahl

Thor Heyerdahl was born in Larvik, Norway, to brewer Thor Senior and Alison Lyng in October 1914. He was intensely passionate about the outdoors and studied zoology and geography in Oslo. He also became interested in Polynesian culture and was given access to Bjarne Kropelien's vast library in the capital.

In 1936 he proposed an expedition to the Pacific islands to learn how animals and plants had arrived there. He spent most of his time on Fatu Hiva, the southernmost of the Marquesas Islands in French Polynesia, which was one of the world's most isolated inhabited islands. He published his account of the expedition in 1938 but the outbreak of war in Europe the following year meant it never entered the public domain.

Based on archaeological evidence and native legends, Heyerdahl suggested that there might have been prehistoric contact between the peoples of South America and Polynesia. Having discovered ancient drawings of Inca rafts by the Conquistadores, he proposed building a balsawood replica and sailing across the Pacific. The raft was christened *Kon-Tiki* after a mythical Incan sun-god and sailed from South America in May 1947. Just over three months later, after a 5,000-mile voyage, the raft ran aground on a reef in the Tuamotu Islands.

His account of the crossing was translated into 70 languages, and the accompanying documentary won an Academy Award in 1951. (A dramatised version released in 2012 was also nominated for an Oscar.) Heyerdahl went against conventional wisdom – which said that Polynesia was colonised from Asia in the west – because there was no other explanation for how the South American sweet potato reached the islands. Indeed, when Admiral Jakob Roggeveen discovered Easter Island in 1722, many of the natives were found to be fair skinned and spoke of their ancestors arriving from the east. There are also similarities between the South American cultures and the islanders in their statues, customs and legends. Heyerdahl visited Easter Island in 1955 and found more anecdotal evidence that the islanders had contact with both early Asian and South American peoples.

In 1969 Heyerdahl set out to cross the Atlantic in a papyrus raft christened *Ra* (after the Egyptian god). Despite making good progress after leaving Morocco, the crew were eventually rescued 100 miles from the Caribbean. The following year, Heyerdahl successfully completed the east–west Atlantic crossing in the *Ra II*. Then, while sailing a reed boat from Iraq to Pakistan, Heyerdahl was denied permission to land anywhere but Djibouti because of the wars in the region. He sent an open letter airing his grievances to UN Secretary-General Kurt Waldheim and then burnt the boat in protest.

He continued to campaign for peace as well as making several exploratory

forays into central Asia in later life. He died from a brain tumour in Italy in 2002 but was then given a state funeral in Oslo Cathedral.

Above: *Thor Heyerdahl*

Sir Edmund Hillary & Tenzing Norgay

Edmund Hillary was born in Auckland, New Zealand, in July 1919 to Percival and Gertrude Hillary. Although intellectually capable, he was initially small in stature so he learned to box to give him confidence. His two-hour train journey to and from high school allowed him time to read and he lapped up adventure stories. At 16, the school organised a field trip to Mount Ruapehu and the now 6'5" Hillary had at last found his vocation. Although he was a little clumsy at first, he had greater endurance and was stronger than his climbing partners.

Having graduated from Auckland University with a maths and science degree, he climbed Mount Ollivier in the Southern Alps. He then took a summer job as a beekeeper, although he continued climbing in the winter. He withdrew an application to sign up for the war effort because of his peaceful nature, but he eventually served as a navigator in the New Zealand Air Force when the Japanese entered the war. Having been injured in a boating accident in Fiji, he was sent home to recover.

In 1948 he climbed Aoraki (Mount Cook) before being invited on an Everest reconnaissance expedition by the British in 1951. As Nepal only allowed one expedition to the mountain each year – and the route through Tibet had been closed by the Chinese – Hillary had to watch and wait while the Swiss made an attempt on the summit in 1952. Tenzing Norgay and Raymond Lambert made it to 8,600 metres before being forced to turn back. The British then recruited Hillary and compatriot George Lowe for an enormous expedition to the Himalayas

in 1953.

Eric Shipton was replaced as team leader by Colonel John Hunt and he organised the assault on the mountain with military precision, each low camp supplying the higher ones until a pyramid of well-stocked camps existed on the mountain's flanks. By the end of May, two summit teams were ready for the final push. But when Charles Evans and Tom Bourdillon had to admit defeat just 91 metres from the summit, the way was clear for Hillary and Tenzing.

Namgyal Wangdi was born to yak herder Ghang La Mingma and Dokmo Kinzom in Khumbu in northeastern Nepal in May 1914. The head lama at the Rongbuk Monastery then suggested he change his name to Ngawang Tenzin Norbu, which became Tenzing Norgay. He considered becoming a monk but eventually decided to join the Sherpa people in Darjeeling.

Shipton recruited him on a 1935 reconnaissance expedition to Everest and he impressed as a high-altitude porter on this and two more trips to the massif in 1936 and 1938. In 1947 he was hired by Canadian Earl Denman to make an illegal attempt on Everest from the Tibetan side but a storm ended their summit bid

a long way short of their target. Having twice been beaten on the mountain with the Swiss in 1952, Tenzing made his seventh trip to Everest with the British the following year.

He saved Hillary's life when the New Zealander slipped into a crevasse early in the expedition, and it was his quick thinking that prompted Hillary to ask Hunt whether he and Tenzing could be paired on a summit assault. When Bourdillon and Evans came up short, Hunt gave Hillary and Tenzing the all-clear to go for the top.

Bad weather delayed them by two days but they eventually established a final high camp at around 8,500 metres. On the morning of May 29th 1953 the two men began their ascent. They soon reached the South Summit and then climbed a tricky 40-foot cliff (thereafter known as the Hillary Step) to open up the final summit ridge. At 11.30am Hillary cut a few more steps in the ice and both men then stood on top of the world.

Hillary wasn't sure Tenzing knew how to work the camera so he took the famous photo of his climbing partner holding his ice axe aloft in triumph. Hillary then took pictures down each ridge to confirm their success, and he also briefly looked for

Opposite: *Hillary in the cockpit of the Trans-Antarctic Expedition's DHC-2 in 1956*

signs that Mallory and Irvine had reached the top in 1924. Finding nothing, the pair returned to the South Col, whereupon Hillary uttered perhaps the most famous line in climbing history (to his great friend George Lowe): "Well, George, we knocked the bastard off!"

News of the successful expedition reached London on the morning of Queen Elizabeth II's coronation, and Hillary and Hunt were knighted for their achievement. Tenzing only received the George Medal, probably because Indian Prime Minister Jawaharal Nehru refused to allow him to be decorated with a knighthood.

Tenzing was elected as the first director of the Himalayan Mountaineering Institute when it was founded in Darjeeling the following year. He also served as a mountain guide for more than 20 years. In 1978 he founded an adventure company that led trekking tours in the Himalayas. He was widely honoured for the rest of his life, and his achievements are still recognised today. This humble but humorous and good-natured adventurer died of a cerebral haemorrhage in Darjeeling in 1986.

Hillary could have basked in the glory of Everest but he climbed 10 more peaks in the Himalayas, as well as becoming the first person for 46 years to reach the South Pole by land. He then made the first crossing of the continent in powered vehicles. He also enjoyed a good slice of

luck throughout his adventuring career: he was late for TWA flight 266, which later crashed in New York after colliding with United 826; and he was supposed to be on an Air New Zealand flight that crashed into Mount Erebus in 1979. His friend, Peter Mulgrew, had taken his place on the latter flight after Hillary was delayed in the US with work commitments. Hillary did suffer great personal loss, however. His wife Louise and daughter Belinda were killed en route to the village of Phaphlu in the Himalayas when their plane crashed near Kathmandu.

Hillary's life and that of the Sherpas remained intertwined for the rest of his life. He founded schools and hospitals in the mountains, using his celebratory to raise the profile of the Himalayan people and help educate their children. When Hillary died in 2008, the world lost a giant of adventure and exploration, as well as one of the greatest New Zealanders and humanitarians.

Amy Johnson

Amy Johnson was born in East Riding, Yorkshire, in July 1903. She went to Boulevard Municipal Secondary School and then graduated from Sheffield University with a degree in economics. She took a position as a solicitor's secretary and then developed a fascination with flying. She soon gained her ground engineer's licence and then, in 1929, her pilot's licence from the London Aeroplane Club.

Her father was unusually supportive and helped buy her a second-hand De Havilland Gipsy Moth, which she christened *Jason* after her father's fish business's trademark. Within a year she had set her sights on becoming the first woman to fly solo non-stop from England to Australia. She left Croydon in South London in May 1930 and stopped first in Vienna. She then hopped across the Middle East, via Constantinople (Istanbul), Aleppo, Baghdad and Bandar Abbas to Karachi, arriving in India on May 10th. By then the wider world had taken notice of her achievements: she was two days ahead of the record set by Australian pioneer Bert Hinkler despite having to cross the Taurus Mountains in Turkey in poor visibility. Indeed on the leg to Aleppo, she came within feet of the mountainside on several occasions, and she then had to make her first emergency landing in the desert after flying into a sandstorm.

She landed heavily at Jhansi the following day and *Jason* had to be repaired, but she then made good time to Calcutta. However, she crashed again after making another emergency landing on a playing field at Insein just north of the Burmese capital Rangoon. The locals

Above: *Jim Mollison and Amy Johnson*

helped retrieve the aircraft from a ditch and soon had it airworthy.

She was then grounded for several days by bad weather, which meant Hinkler's record couldn't be broken, but she eventually landed in Darwin after an 11,000-mile journey on May 24th. The flight had been extensively covered in the Australian media and she was feted for six weeks. In fact she was so exhausted by all the attention that she returned home by sea to Port Said before taking an Imperial Airways flight to Croydon. A crowd of nearly a million people lined her route into London.

In 1931 Johnson was ready for another challenge and she became the first pilot to fly from London to Moscow in a day. She and co-pilot Jack Humphreys then continued through Siberia to Japan, breaking more records in the process. She married renowned aviator Jim Mollison in 1932 and promptly broke his record from London to Cape Town. She and Mollison then received a ticker-tape parade through New York after flying non-stop from Wales to Connecticut. The pair then broke the record for the shortest flight time from Britain to India as part of the MacRobertson Air Race. Johnson's last record-breaking flight was made between Britain and South Africa in a Percival Gull in 1936.

By 1940 she had divorced Mollison and joined the Air Transport Auxiliary to help with the war effort. She soon rose to the rank of first officer while transporting aircraft and personnel around the country. In January 1941 she was flying an Airspeed Oxford from Blackpool to RAF Kidlington when she lost her bearings in poor weather. Her plane apparently ran out of fuel and crashed in the Thames Estuary, although Johnson was seen bailing out so the crew of HMS *Haslemere* tried to rescue her. Lieutenant Commander Walter Fletcher dived in to help her back to the ship but he drowned in the rescue attempt and Johnson's body was never found.

This may be the official version but a number of witnesses have since come forward to say that Amy Johnson's aircraft was misidentified and shot down by the Royal Navy. In 1999 Tom Mitchell claimed that he'd fired 16 anti-aircraft shells at the Airspeed Oxford because the pilot gave the wrong identification code for that day (usually a colour). The crew of the *Haslemere* all believed it was an enemy aircraft until they saw the papers the following day. Their superiors then swore them to secrecy because Johnson was rumoured to be carrying a VIP (whose identity has never been established).

Amy Johnson was England's Amelia Earhart. She was widely decorated during her flying career and broke numerous speed and distance records. She has had several songs written about her and films made about her life. Many schools and public buildings are named after her, and a number of statues have been erected in her memory. She remains one of the greatest female pilots of all time.

Meriwether Lewis & William Clark

Meriwether Lewis was born to William and Lucy (both of British descent) in Virginia in August 1774. His father died when he was young so his stepfather, Captain John Marks, moved the family to Georgia in 1780. He had no formal schooling until his teens but he became a skilled hunter who developed a passion for natural history. Lewis also seems to have championed the cause of the Cherokee Indians from a young age.

Having been sent back to Virginia to complete his education, he graduated from Liberty Hall in Washington and then joined the Virginia militia that quelled the 1794 Whiskey Rebellion. He signed up for the army in 1795 and left as a captain in 1801 (one of his commanding officers was William Clark). He was then approached by President Thomas Jefferson – who he knew through acquaintances in Virginia

society – to organise an expedition across the continent to estimate the extent and value of the land to the west (and its resources), to find a navigable watercourse across the country, to declare American sovereignty over Native Americans living in the Missouri river valley, and to assess whether a trade route could be established with the Far East.

As the United States had just bought nearly a million square miles of land from the French (the Louisiana Purchase), Jefferson was keen to extend the US's sphere of influence all the way to the Pacific Ocean between the Spanish-held lands to the south and Canada to the north. Lewis agreed to the two-year trans-continental expedition as long as it was co-led by William Clark.

William was born in Virginia to John and Ann Clark in August 1770. The family owned several small estates and Clark was schooled at home. He was too young to serve but his brothers fought in the Revolutionary War (1775-1783) before the family moved to Kentucky. In 1789 Clark volunteered to fight against the American Indians north of the Ohio River (during which he kept a journal) and he was involved in several campaigns before the decisive Battle of Fallen Timbers in 1794 that ended the Northwest Indian War. He resigned his commission two years later due to illness but accepted Lewis's invitation to command the Corps of Discovery on its expedition west. Time was of the essence because Alexander MacKenzie had already crossed Canada to the west coast and there was a danger that the British would try to seize control of any fur trade route.

Lewis and Clark convened near Louisville in October 1803 and departed with nine men later in the month. They carried medals of peace declaring sovereignty over the indigenous people as well as weapons of war should they be opposed. They also carried medical supplies and cases of scientific equipment to make and record their observations. The team took on more people and supplies at Camp Dubois on the east bank of the Mississippi in Illinois before following the Missouri westwards.

Having passed La Charrette, the last white settlement on the river, they continued following the watercourse through what are now the states of Kansas, Missouri, Omaha, Nebraska and Iowa. In August 1804 they finally reached the Great Plains in the middle of the continental landmass. Although the plains teemed with elk and bison, the party relied on Indian hospitality and guidance to see them through a harsh winter. The Sioux and several more tribes weren't as accommodating but shrewd diplomacy

from Lewis and Clark meant they never had to fight.

The party crossed the continental divide and then canoed along the Clearwater, Snake and Columbia Rivers to what is now Portland in Oregon. Upon sighting Mount Hood, they realised they were close to the Pacific, which they then reached in the coming weeks. They wintered in a fort before heading for home by canoeing back up the Columbia River.

Despite running into trouble with several Indian tribes on the return journey, they reached St Louis in September 1806. They had achieved their objective of reaching the Pacific Ocean, and they had also established trading contracts with many of the 70 previously unknown indigenous tribes, but they hadn't found a continuous watercourse across the continent. They did, however, produce extraordinary maps of the Pacific Northwest, and they were the first Americans to cross the continental divide, traverse Yellowstone and enter Montana.

Jefferson was delighted with the results of the expedition: he used seeds they brought back to grow Indian corn; he announced US rule over the new territories; and he believed that the maps opened the door to later expeditions of discovery. He then

gave Lewis 1,600 acres of land and made him Governor of Louisiana.

Lewis brokered peace deals between many of the Indian tribes but found it difficult to work alongside local politicians. While on a trip to Washington in 1809, Lewis stayed overnight at an inn near Nashville. Witnesses heard gunshots just before dawn and Lewis was pronounced dead later that morning. It isn't clear if he was murdered or committed suicide.

Clark was appointed brigadier-general of the Louisiana Militia in 1807 and Governor of the Missouri Territory in 1813. His position meant he was charged with forcing the Indian tribes to cede to the United States but his conscience couldn't allow them to become extinct and he was often said to be too compassionate. He ended up trying to protect their culture and preserve their identity, history and language, while at the same time encouraging them to adopt a federal existence. In 1822 he was appointed as Superintendent of Indian affairs, a position he held until his death in 1838.

The Lewis and Clark Expedition opened up the United States to future traders and adventurers, and their status as the greatest American explorers remains intact.

Opposite: *William Clark*

Ferdinand Magellan & Juan Sebastián Elcano

Ferdinand Magellan was born in around 1480 but his place of birth is disputed: it was either on the outskirts of Porto or at Vila Real in Portugal. His parents were Rodrigo de Magalhães and Alda de Mesquita, although they both died while he was a youngster. Because of their social standing, Magellan became a pageboy at the royal court of Queen Leonor.

When he was 25, Magellan signed up to travel east with the fleet of the first Portuguese Viceroy of India. He spent eight years on the subcontinent, fighting with distinction and eventually helping to conquer Malacca on the Malaysian Peninsula in 1511. Having been rewarded with vast riches, his reputation then suffered after he was injured in Morocco and then accused of trading with the Moors in the Mediterranean.

He received the odd offer to join trading ships but had his heart set on reaching the Spice Islands by sailing west around the tip of South America rather than east around the Cape of Good Hope. In 1517 Magellan presented his plan to Charles I of Spain: if he could reach the islands by sailing west into the newly discovered Pacific Ocean, it wouldn't conflict with the Portuguese who had claimed the eastern route for themselves.

Magellan and partner Rui Faleiro were supplied with ships and crew and funded by the Spanish crown. Faleiro decided not to travel at the last minute so Magellan took on Juan Sebastián Elcano, a merchant ship captain seeking a royal pardon. Despite several teething problems during preparation – opposition from the Portuguese and a lack of funds – Magellan eventually led the five-ship fleet

(flagship *Trinidad* as well as *San Antonio*, *Concepción*, *Santiago* and *Victoria*) from Seville in August 1519.

King Manuel I ordered the Portuguese navy to give chase but Magellan easily eluded them. The fleet stopped briefly in the Canary Islands before departing Cape Verde for Rio de Janeiro. As Brazil was a Portuguese territory, Magellan stayed offshore before heading south to look for a strait linking the two oceans. He quelled a mutiny over Easter in 1520 (the mutineers were impaled and left on the coast, and their remains were later found by Sir Francis Drake) but then lost the *Santiago* in a storm. The captain of the *San Antonio* then deserted and sailed back to Spain.

Magellan eventually navigated the treacherous strait at the tip of South America and his three remaining ships entered the Pacific Ocean. The fleet continued northwest and reached the Mariana Islands on March 6th 1521. Two weeks later, he sailed to Homonhon in the Philippines. Some of the native people were friendly but Magellan felt that the rest needed to be converted to Christianity.

Lapu-Lapu resisted the colonisation of Mactan and assembled an army to defend the island when Magellan's party approached. During the ensuing battle between 49 Spanish sailors and as many as 1,000 natives, Magellan was struck in the face with a bamboo spear. He was then finished off by a crowd of locals, and Lapu-Lapu refused to return his body.

The Spanish force had been decimated and there were too few left alive to sail

Above: *Ferdinand Magellan*

Spain

Atlantic Ocean

ific Ocean

Magellan died here
April 27, 1521

Philippine Islands

Strait of Magellan

Above: *The Magellan-Elcano circumnavigation of the globe*

all three ships. The *Concepción* was burned and the remaining two ships, *Trinidad* and *Victoria*, then sailed on to Brunei and Borneo before eventually reaching the Spice Islands in November. Having traded goods for spices with the Sultan of Tidore, the ships headed into the Indian Ocean for the voyage home. *Trinidad* was found to be unseaworthy however, so it was rerouted east and was eventually captured by the Portuguese.

The *Victoria* under Juan Sebastián Elcano continued heading west towards the Cape of Good Hope. Despite losing men to starvation and abandoning others

lest they lose their cargo of spices, Elcano finally arrived back in Spain in September 1522 after an epic three-year voyage of discovery. The original plan had only involved finding a new route to the Spice Islands but because Elcano had continued westwards the *Victoria* had completed the first circumnavigation of the Earth. Only 18 men of her original crew of 237 had survived the journey. Elcano died of malnutrition on an expedition to occupy the Spice Islands in 1525.

Aside from visiting new lands, navigating uncharted waters and identifying new plant and animal species,

Left: *Juan Sebastián Elcano*

the expedition's lasting legacy was the International Date Line. The crew kept extremely accurate logs and realised on their return that their date was a day behind because they had travelled west against the planet's direction of rotation. This seemed extraordinary and a special delegation had to be sent to the Pope to explain the anomaly. Having covered more than 37,000 miles, the expedition also established the true extent of the Earth.

Magellan remains one of the most honoured explorers in recorded history. Elcano, however, is too often overlooked even though he was the skipper who brought the *Victoria* home to Spain after its epic voyage around the world.

George Mallory & Andrew Irvine

Some might not consider mountaineers to be explorers in the traditional sense, but the great polar explorers and early 20th-century adventurers always considered Mount Everest to be the 'third pole'. Indeed Mallory's 1921 expedition to the Himalayas was more about mapping the area around the mountain than making an attempt on its summit.

George Mallory was born in Cheshire in 1886 to Herbert, a clergyman, and Annie, the daughter of a clergyman. He won a maths scholarship to Winchester in 1899, where he met Robert Irving, a schoolmaster and mountaineer who organised climbing trips to the Alps each year. Mallory proved to be an outstanding rock climber who then pioneered several extremely difficult routes in the Lake District.

He graduated with a history degree from Cambridge in 1908 and then took up teaching at Charterhouse in Surrey. There he met wife Ruth and they married just a week before the outbreak of the First World War. He fought in the conflict and remained largely unaffected by the horrors. He then returned to Charterhouse after the war and signed up for the first British expedition to Everest in 1921.

With the help of a dozen Sherpas, Mallory discovered the Rongbuk Glacier that led to the sheer North Face of Everest, as well as being the first westerner to see the Lhotse Face and Western Cwm. He also climbed several peaks in the massif and finally stumbled across the East Rongbuk Glacier, which is now used by all climbers from the Tibetan side of the mountain as the route to the summit.

Mallory then climbed the 7,000-metre saddle of the North Col to plan a route up the Northeast Ridge.

Mallory returned the following year to make a serious attempt on the mountain. He, Howard Somervell and Edward Norton reached the crest of the ridge at 8,225 metres before turning back exhausted. A second attempt by George Finch used oxygen and climbed much faster, reaching 8,300 metres before being forced down by bad weather. Mallory organised a final attempt as the monsoon approached, but an avalanche swept away seven Sherpa porters and the attempt was abandoned. Mallory shouldered the blame for the accident and it was difficult for him to return to the Himalayas for another attempt in 1924. On his final expedition to Everest, he met Andrew Irvine.

Irvine was born in Birkenhead in 1902 to William and Lilian. He studied at Shrewsbury School where he showed great promise as an engineer. While aged only 13 he submitted a design to the War Office for a gearing mechanism that would allow a machinegun to be fired through the propeller blades of an aircraft without hitting them.

He was a star oarsman who won

Above: *George Mallory and wife Ruth*

the boat race in 1923 while studying engineering at Oxford, and he then joined the university's mountaineering club. He joined the Merton College Arctic Expedition to Spitsbergen in 1923 and, as he seemed competent in every aspect of climbing and survival, Noel Odell asked him to join the 1924 expedition to Mount Everest. Irvine and Mallory ended

up sharing a cabin aboard the *SS California* as it sailed for India from Liverpool.

The two men became close friends on the long trek inland to Everest. By February they'd reached Darjeeling and selected their porters, but it wasn't until the end of April that they'd established their base camp in the Rongbuk Valley. Over the next month they established more camps on the mountain. On June 1st Mallory and Geoffrey Bruce made a summit attempt but their porters abandoned them before they could establish a high camp and they had to abort.

The following day Edward Norton and Howard Somervell began their summit attempt. They soon established a high camp, which they left on the morning of June 4th but Somervell was forced to turn back at midday (he coughed up the lining of his larynx on the descent only moments before suffocating). Norton continued alone and eventually established a world altitude record of 8,570 metres that wasn't officially broken until the Swiss reached 8,611 metres in 1952. But, due to a mixture of exhaustion, altitude sickness and the difficulty of the terrain, Norton too had to accept defeat.

A third and final attempt was organised by Mallory two days later. Rather than climbing with the experienced Noel Odell, Mallory chose Irvine. It is a decision that has perplexed historians ever since but Odell was a notoriously slow starter in the mornings and, now that Mallory had become convinced by the beneficial effects of climbing with oxygen, the more practical Irvine (who'd all but invented a completely new and reliable oxygen system) was the logical choice. The younger man probably wouldn't question Mallory's decisions on the mountain either, whereas Odell might.

On the morning of June 8th Mallory and Irvine left their high camp and climbed towards immortality. At 12.50pm the clouds cleared and they were seen from below by Odell at what he believed was the difficult second rock step

on the ridge. Odell claimed they climbed it in five minutes before pushing hard for the summit. Then the cloud rolled in and they were never seen again.

In the intervening years, contradictory evidence has come to light about what happened to Mallory and Irvine. It is impossible to climb the notoriously difficult second step in five minutes so Odell's sighting is unreliable. However, he was a trained geologist with an eye for detail so he probably mistook their location on the ridge rather than imagining the sighting itself. An oxygen bottle and ice axe were subsequently found just below the easier first step, and Mallory's body was eventually found in 1999 on a fall line well below their likely final position. This indicates that the accident almost certainly happened on the descent (as most do), and that it happened at night (Mallory's sunglasses were in his pocket). His torso is marked with rope-jerk injuries indicating the men were still together when one of them fell. His injuries are relatively minor compared with those of the other climbers in the area, suggesting that he and Irvine had climbed down from the ridge and were crossing treacherous roof-tile-like rocks on the face instead.

Mallory had said that he'd leave a picture of Ruth on the summit, and there was no sign of the photo on his body, but Mallory was notoriously forgetful and he could easily have misplaced it during the long expedition. There was no sign of the camera either, which means the ever-dependable Irvine was probably carrying it. Until his body is found – there have been several possible sightings – none of these questions can be answered definitively. The general consensus among the climbing community is that the second step was just beyond Mallory's climbing capability and there was no way Irvine could have climbed it without help. The romantics still believe that Mallory might have gone on alone to the summit before returning to join Irvine, although it's almost certain that he would have been climbing without oxygen for the final summit pyramid, a feat not managed for certain until Reinhold Messner's incredible solo oxygen-less climb in 1980.

The motivation for the climb has

long-been debated but it seems certain that restoring national pride by lifting the people's spirits after the Great War was the driving force. The British had already mounted unsuccessful missions to both poles, and then Captain Scott had died in Antarctica days after discovering Roald Amundsen had beaten him to the South Pole. With the North Pole having apparently been reached by the American explorer Robert Peary in 1909, only Everest remained.

With the loss of Mallory and Irvine, the British climbing scene went into decline for almost a decade, and it wasn't until 1933 that a serious expedition returned to the mountain. It would be another 20 years, however, before Everest was finally climbed for certain. Although the 1953 expedition was organised by the British and led by Colonel John Hunt, New Zealander Edmund Hillary and Sherpa Tenzing Norgay were the first men to set foot on the summit. They looked for evidence of Mallory and Irvine but found nothing.

Robert Peary, Frederick Cook, Ralph Plaisted & Walter Herbert

Never in the field of human exploration has there been as much controversy as that which surrounded the exploits of Peary and Cook, and it was eventually left to Plaisted and Herbert to pick up the pieces.

Rear Admiral Robert Peary was born in Pennsylvania to Charles and Mary in May 1856. Charles died while Robert was an infant so Mary moved the family to Portland. He went to Bowdoin College and eventually graduated in 1877 with a degree in civil engineering. He initially worked as a draftsman but then joined the navy in 1881 as a lieutenant. In 1885 his diary indicates that he'd decided to become the first man to reach the geographic North Pole. He then wrote a paper proposing two ways it could be done, and by 1886 he had mounted his first expedition.

Having only penetrated 100 miles east from Godhavn on Disko Island off Greenland, Peary suddenly became aware of the magnitude of the undertaking. When he returned home, he was dispatched to Nicaragua by the navy to survey routes for a canal linking the Atlantic and Pacific Oceans. During preparation for the trip he met Matthew Henson, and the former sales assistant was soon recruited to Peary's polar team.

In 1891, Peary gained backing from several academic institutions to mount another expedition by his second route. During the trip his ship's tiller spun unexpectedly and broke Peary's lower leg. On the advice of Doctor Frederick Cook, who had been hired as the party's surgeon, Peary recuperated at a camp built by the team. By 1892 he was fit enough to mount several short excursions onto the ice, and he concluded that Greenland must be an island.

Two more expeditions – in 1898 and 1905 – began to reveal inconsistencies between notes made in his dairies and those recorded afterwards however. In 1906, for example, he claimed to have reached 87°06'N before returning overnight to 86°30' without camping, a distance of 72 miles in a day when most expeditions averaged 10. And on June 24th 1906 his diary noted 'no land visible' while in a later book he claimed to have discovered land on that day. In 1914, Donald MacMillan's expedition found no land at Peary's reported position.

The greatest threat to any explorer's reputation was credibility, as both Peary and Cook were about to find out.

Frederick Cook was born in June 1865 in New York to Theodore and Magdalena Koch. He went to Columbia University and received his doctorate

Above: *Robert Peary in 1909*

from New York University Medical School in 1890. He was the surgeon on Peary's 1891 expedition to the Arctic and he also joined the Belgian Antarctic Expedition in 1897, during which he formed a lifelong bond with Roald Amundsen.

During a subsequent trip to Tierra del Fuego, Cook borrowed a dictionary of the local language written by missionary Thomas Bridges. When Bridges died the following year, Cook tried to pass the

work off as his own. Then, in 1906, Cook claimed to have reached the summit of Denali (Mount McKinley), the highest mountain in North America. Although some members of his team expressed doubts privately, no public criticism was aired until 1909 when Cook and Peary came to blows over who had reached the North Pole first. When Cook's maps and photos from the mountaineering expedition were then analysed, they were found to bear no resemblance to the summit. Indeed his summit photo was actually taken on what became known as Fake Peak 19 miles away.

Cook's trip to the Arctic in 1907 ended equally controversially. Having stayed for the winter in Annoatok in northern Greenland, he set off for the pole in February 1908. Travelling with only two Inuit, he claimed to have reached the North Pole on April 22nd 1908. Having endured a torrid return journey, the three men finally made it back to Annoatok in early 1909, just as Peary was on his way to the pole.

Cook's navigational readings have been largely discredited since, and the accounts of the two Inuit bear a striking resemblance to the fictional journey taken by the explorers in Jules Verne's 1864 novel *The English at the North Pole*. Much of his data was left in three wooden caskets in the care of hunter Harry Whitney. When Whitney asked Peary to bring the cases back to America on the *Roosevelt* in 1909, Peary refused and ordered the cases to be buried in the ice.

With Peary launching a sustained attack on Cook's reputation, and the recently discovered fraud concerning his mountaineering achievements in Alaska casting more doubt on him, Cook never recovered his credibility. He was imprisoned for seven years for fraud in 1923 (the judge was a friend of the Peary family) but was later pardoned by President Roosevelt. He died in 1940, leaving Peary to claim the credit for being the first man to reach the North Pole. It is a sad fact that his confirmed discovery of Meighen Island and his remarkable survival in the Arctic using Inuit techniques were all but forgotten.

Peary's claims have also come under scrutiny, however.

He and his team left New York aboard the ice ship *Roosevelt* in July 1908. They spent the winter on Ellesmere Island before leaving for the pole at the end of February using the Peary relay system of leaving supply caches. On March 31st Peary made camp at 87°45'N (133 miles from the pole) and sent back everyone but Henson and four Inuit, none of whom could navigate and confirm their position. He then maintained an average of 26 miles per day (when previously he'd managed 13 at best) before taking a navigational reading that confirmed he was only three miles from his target.

On April 6th 1909 Peary made several

Above: *Peary's picture of his team at the North Pole*

exploratory trips for up to 10 miles across the ice to ensure he'd reached the pole itself (the ice drifts on the surface currents). However, he didn't write about the event immediately – the two days he allegedly spent at the pole are blank in his diary and a separate sheet records his famous line 'The Pole at last!!' – and his behaviour during the return to the *Roosevelt* was oddly subdued. Four months later, Peary

finally sent a telegraph stating that the Stars and Stripes had been nailed to the North Pole. He then received a reply that Cook had got there first.

Cook's reputation soon lay in tatters however, and Peary, with his depth soundings and photographic evidence (the angle of the sun in his images can be used to determine latitude), was declared the discoverer of the pole. However, the images don't give a precise location because the shadows are indistinct, and Peary – who knew the images could verify his claim – took no photos on flat ground that would have confirmed his position beyond doubt. His depth soundings are accurate close to land but he never touched the bottom in the higher latitudes so his readings don't give a detailed picture of the seafloor. He also refused to sanction an investigation into his trip or release all his evidence. Therefore, the experienced Danish panel that had analysed and then debunked Cook's claim couldn't judge Peary's. The American Geographic Society refused to recognise the achievement, primarily due to the inconsistent speeds claimed by Peary on the final push.

On their return to the camp where he'd left experienced navigator Bob Bartlett, his speed increased further because he made the 133-mile journey in two and a half days, contradicting the account of the trip by Henson who claimed they'd made slow progress on the final leg because of tortuous detours to avoid pressure ridges and open water. British explorer Tom Avery attempted to resolve the issue in 2005 when he recreated Peary's trip with period clothing, equipment, loads and method of transport. They reached the pole in just short of 37 days, five hours faster than Peary. This seemed to confirm that Peary had indeed been successful, but in fact it casts more doubt on his claim because he was held up by open water for five days, and Avery never managed more than 90 miles in any five-day stretch. Avery also knew his team would be airlifted to safety from the pole so they carried far fewer supplies.

On balance, it seems that if Peary wasn't actually at the North Pole on April 6th, he must have been within 50 miles or so.

Because the wider world was convinced that either Cook or Peary had reached the pole, there was no value in trekking there on foot in the years immediately afterwards. Roald Amundsen certainly crossed the pole in an airship in 1926 but it wasn't until

Above: *Sir Walter Herbert*

American Ralph Plaisted took a ski-doo to the pole in 1968 that a surface crossing was indisputably achieved. In 1969 British explorer Walter 'Wally' Herbert led an unpowered surface expedition and was thus the first person to have definitely walked to the North Pole. He later wrote a book criticising Peary for falsifying his records, although, as has been mentioned, recent reviews of the evidence suggest Peary was extremely close to the pole when his data were taken.

Marco Polo

Marco Polo was born in Venice in September 1254. His father, Niccolò, was a wealthy merchant who traded with the Turks. Niccolò and his brother, Maffeo, foresaw the collapse of Constantinople and liquidated their assets before travelling into Asia and being received by the Kublai Khan. Marco's mother, meanwhile, died so he was raised by an aunt and uncle (Niccolò didn't meet his son until he returned in 1269).

When he was just 17, Marco joined his father and uncle for another trek into Asia. They didn't return for 24 years having travelled 15,000 miles across and around the continent by land and sea. Marco Polo chronicled his incredible journey in a manuscript, although some of his claims have been disputed ever since.

His narrative begins with his father's previous journey, during which Niccolò and Maffeo reportedly reached Beijing (then called Dadu). There the Kublai Khan seemed fascinated by the European legal system, the Pope and the church, as well as the arts, maths and culture of their homeland. Kublai Khan asked Niccolò to head back to Europe and deliver a letter to the Pope. He also asked that he return with anointing oil from Jerusalem. Niccolò and Maffeo carried out the Kublai Khan's wishes and, with a young Marco, they left Italy with the Pope's reply in 1271.

They first sailed to Acre in Israel before crossing the desert of present-day Iraq and Iran to Hormuz. There they were to have boarded ships bound for China but the vessels weren't seaworthy so the Polos continued overland for the

3,000-mile journey to Shangdu. Finally, in around 1275, the family returned to the Kublai Khan and delivered the Pope's reply and the sacred oil.

Kublai Khan then denied the family permission to leave China, although Marco, who was fluent in four languages and who had absorbed many of the customs of the Mongol people, was recruited as a government official. He travelled widely in southern China and even visited Burma. The Polos were eventually allowed to accompany Kublai's great-nephew as he returned home to Persia after visiting China in search of a wife.

The two-year voyage from Zaitun to Singapore, Sumatra, Jaffna, Pandyan and eventually back to Hormuz was so arduous that only 18 of the original party of 600 survived (although Niccolò, Maffeo and Marco were among them). Having reached Hormuz, the family left the remains of the wedding party and journeyed overland to the Black Sea port of Trebizond.

tissimū b3 qui nulli tributarī ē Woles insule ydolatre sūt
et oēs nude ābulant mares et femine ß quilib3 verecūda
opit páno vno Nullū bladū bñt excepto riso Carnib° ri
so et lacte viuūt babūdanciā bñt seminū solūmo de quib°
oleū faciūt bñt biricios meliores mūdi qui ibi crescūt Ali
nū eciā bñt de arborib° de quib° dm̄ ē sup in regno sama
rā In bac isula lapides pciosi iueniūr qui dicūt Rubini
qui regionib° alijs nō inueniūt vel bñt . Multi eni eciā
sapbiri et topacij et amatiste ibi sunt multiq3 alij lapides p
ciosi Rex buius insule baberpulcbriorē rubinū qui vnq̄
fuit visus in boc mūdo babet enim vni° palme longitudi
né et ad mensurā grossiciei bracbij bois Est āt splendid°
sup modū omni macula carens adeo vt ignis ardens vide
atur esse Magn° kaam Cublay nuncios suos direxit ad
illū rogans vt prefatū lapidē illi donaret et ipe donaret ei
valore vnīus ciuitatis D. ni m̄dit q̄ lapis ille snoz erat añ
cessorū nulli eū vmq̄ homini daret Hui° insule boies bel
licosi non sunt sed valde viles D. uando autē bella cū alig
bus babent de alienis ptibus stipendiarios vocant et spe
cialiter sarracenos

De regno maabar   Capitulū xxiij.

Ltra insulā seylā ad mītiaria xl iuenif maabarq̄ ma
ior india nūcupat Nō sūt ē insula ß terra firma. In
bac puincia quiq3 reges sūt Prouicia ē nobilissia et ditis
sima sup modū In pmo bui° puicie rex ē noīe Seudeba
i quo regno sūt margarite i copia maxiā In mari eni bui°
puincie ē maris bracbiū seu sinus inē firmā terrā et insulā
q̄dā vbi nō est aquaz pfūdites vltra decem vel duodecī
passus et alicubi vltra duos Ibi inueniūt margarite sup
dce Mercatores eni diuersi societates adinuice faciunt τ
bñt naues magnas et puas boiesq3 cōbucuut qui descen
dūt ad pfūdū aquarū et capiunt cōcbilia in quibus sunt

margarite D. ñ autē bij
dunt rursūq3 descendūt
aūt in sinu illo maris pis
cendentes in mare sed p
culo puidetur cōbucunt
dicūtur Abrayanna qui
abolica cogunt et stupe
possint ledere Et quia b
nocte fit magi illi de die
nocte dissoluunt Timen
rū licencia mare descend
aūt metuentes in mare a
alius inuenitur qui sciat
nisi illi abrayanna quia
piscacio i mari sit p totū
sis may et tūc de margar
do quas negociatores p
gociatores aūt qui band
de omnibus margaritis
cantatoribus aūt qui stu
simū ptem piscatoribus
vero may vlteri° nō rep
isto p ccc miliaria distat
mēsem septēbris ysq3 m
buius puincie pplus o
tñ vno verecūdia opit
vt alij sed ad collū deser
et rubinis alijs q3 precio
q̄ torques est maximi pc
collū eius torda de serie
lapides preciosi margar
Oportet enim cū singul
dicere de mane ad deor

Although Marco Polo wasn't the first European to visit China, his writings were the first to chronicle the journey and the people he encountered. Such was his influence that Christopher Columbus had a copy of the book (with accompanying handwritten notes) listed amongst his possessions. Polo's travels also influenced the way new territories were mapped, which no doubt influenced the great European voyages of exploration over the coming centuries.

He returned to Venice in 1295 with a fortune in precious stones, but he found his home at war with Genoa. Polo equipped a galley with a trebuchet (enormous slingshot catapult) and fought in skirmishes off the Anatolian Coast, although he was captured the following year. While imprisoned, he dictated an account of his epic journey to fellow inmate Rustichello da Pisa, and the manuscript eventually appeared as *The Travels of Marco Polo*.

He was released in 1299 and returned to Venice a wealthy man, which allowed him to finance more expeditions, although he never left the city again. He married Donata Badoer the following year and she bore him three daughters. He died in January 1324 at the age of 69.

Left: *Marco Polo's book is annotated by Christopher Columbus*

Captain Robert Scott

Robert Falcon Scott was born in Devon in 1868 to John and Hannah. His father may have been a brewer and local magistrate but Scott had four uncles serving in the military and the youngster was sent to Stubbington House in Hampshire to prepare him for life in the navy. In 1881 he passed his entrance exams and began his career as a cadet, and by 1883 he was a midshipman on HMS *Boadicea*.

Four years later, while serving on HMS *Rover* in the West Indies, he met Clements Markham, Secretary of the Royal Geographic Society (RGS). Markham was impressed with the young man's intelligence and enthusiasm and made a note of his name. Scott's naval career, meanwhile, progressed smoothly, although three months of his service record are missing from the admiralty's

documents and he did earn a mild rebuke for grounding a torpedo boat.

His father soon declared himself bankrupt and died shortly after taking a new job, and then Scott's brother, Archie, who'd taken a higher-paid job to support the family, also died after contracting typhoid. The family now relied solely on Scott for income so he applied to lead the RGS's Antarctic expedition aboard *Discovery*. Markham appointed him as commander and the ship sailed in August 1901.

The crew was woefully inexperienced in Antarctic survival, however, and the long journey south across the ice cap by Scott, Ernest Shackleton and Edward Wilson, while taking them to within 550 miles of the South Pole, almost proved fatal on the return when they battled the extreme cold and starvation. Shackleton was particularly ill so Scott sent him home. (Despite people believing this to be the point at which the men fell out, Scott welcomed Shackleton home after his 1909 *Nimrod* expedition and the two were still exchanging polite letters the following year.)

Discovery made it home in 1904 and Scott was feted as a national hero. He spent the next year receiving honours, giving lectures and writing up the expedition for publication. Two years later he resumed his illustrious naval career as Assistant Director of Naval Intelligence. In 1907 he met sculptress Kathleen Bruce and they married the following year.

When Shackleton returned home from Antarctica in triumphant failure, Scott saw the opportunity to steal his rival's thunder and be the first to the South Pole. In 1910 his ship, the *Terra Nova*, sailed south but it wasn't until he received a telegram from Roald Amundsen while he was in Melbourne that Scott realised he was in a race for the pole.

Scott was still convinced that man-hauling sledges laden with supplies was the quickest way to cross the ice. Shackleton had tried using motor-sleds and horses but both proved inadequate. Neither man was particularly taken with dog-sledding,

Above: *Captain Robert Falcon Scott*

although the Norwegians and Inuit knew it the fastest and most economical way to cross the ice caps as long as the dog handlers were well trained, which in this case they weren't. Scott's complex assault involved horses, motor-sleds and dogs, although the Siberian horses weren't cut out for the work and were soon shot, while the motor-sleds were equally useless.

Having finally established a supply

Above: *Scott's despondent team pose at the South Pole in January 1912. They would all perish on the return journey*

depot at around 80°S, Scott's team returned to their base and learned that Amundsen had landed with a huge pack of dogs 200 miles to the east. Scott refused to adapt his plans because he was travelling a known route, and his large polar team departed on November 1st 1911. As they headed south, men from the supporting teams gradually turned back so the assault party would have enough food to make a dash for the pole.

By January 1912 eight men had reached 87°34'S. Scott sent Teddy Evans, William Lashly and Tom Crean back, while he, Edward Wilson, Henry Bowers, Lawrence Oates and Edgar Evans pushed on. Two weeks later the exhausted party reached the South Pole, only to find that

Amundsen had beaten them to it by five weeks. Scott's diary entry says it all: *The worst has happened. All the daydreams must go. Great God, this is an awful place.*

They spent a day at the pole before beginning the 800-mile return journey across the most inhospitable terrain on the planet. They initially made good progress and by mid-February were halfway to safety. Edgar Evans's condition then deteriorated rapidly and he died after a fall on February 17th. Despite Scott's earlier orders for the support party to head south and meet them on March 1st, many of the would-be rescuers also needed medical attention or decided to continue their scientific observations. These were fatal miscalculations.

Scott's party were now in a desperate situation so Captain Oates voluntarily left the tent to give the others a better chance of survival. The rest were now at the mercy of snow blindness, frostbite, hunger and exhaustion, and the worsening weather. Scott, Wilson and Bowers made their final camp on March 19th just 11 miles from their food depot. They were trapped by the weather for another nine days and eventually died from malnutrition and exposure.

A search party discovered their camp in November but news of the tragedy didn't filter out until the *Terra Nova* reached New Zealand in February 1913. Scott received glowing tributes in the world's press and monuments were erected to him across the UK but history hasn't been as kind to him.

His reputation survived until after the Second World War but then a series of biographies questioned his leadership, planning and man management, the most damning of which was Roland Huntford's in 1979. This decline in his reputation coincided with a dramatic reversal in fortune for his long-time rival Ernest Shackleton. Shackleton's reputation had initially been overshadowed by Scott, but when Scott's failings were aired in public via various books, Shackleton's incredible open-boat journey and subsequent rescue of his men took on mythic proportions. Indeed, in a 2002 poll to find the greatest Britons, Shackleton came 11th and Scott a lowly 54th.

The new century has been kinder to Scott, however. Bad luck, appalling weather and a support team who failed him doubtless contributed to the poor publicity, while his leadership under extreme circumstances should now survive the test of time.

Sir Ernest Shackleton

Opposite:
Shackleton at 27

Ernest Shackleton was born in February 1874 in County Kildare, Ireland, to Henry and Henrietta. He was the second of 10 children. (His younger brother, Frank, was accused and then acquitted of the theft of Ireland's crown jewels in 1907.) Henry moved to Dublin to study medicine in 1880 and then took the family to suburban London to look for work four years later.

Ernest was initially home-schooled – he was an avid reader who devoured adventure books – before enrolling at Fir Lodge School in Dulwich. At Dulwich College he seemed bored by schoolwork and led an undistinguished youth, although he had enough natural intelligence to see him through his studies.

He left college at 16 and went to sea as an apprentice on the sailing ship *Hoghton Tower* because his father couldn't afford the cadet's berth on a navy or merchant ship. He spent four years travelling the world, learning his trade and forming lasting relationships with people of all classes and means. By 1898 he was a qualified master mariner capable of skippering any British ship. As a young, sympathetic and competent officer, he joined the Union-Castle Line, transporting mail and passengers to South Africa. At the outbreak of the Boer War he transferred to a troop ship and met Lieutenant Cedric Longstaff whose father was a backer of the National Antarctic Expedition.

Shackleton used his connection to secure a commission as a sub-lieutenant in the navy, which led to a place as third officer on the *Discovery* for its journey south in 1901. The expedition was led by Commander Robert Falcon Scott who, as an ex-navy man, ran a tight ship under

Right:
*Shackleton's ship
Endurance is
crushed by the ice*

navy rules. Although Shackleton accepted this style of leadership, he preferred the more relaxed attitude of officers in the merchant navy.

There were rumours that Shackleton had eyes on leading the expedition but this seems unlikely as Scott chose him to join an exploratory mission south towards the pole, which indicated a level of trust between them. It was an extremely arduous trip that saw all 22 dogs die and the three men suffer from snow blindness, frostbite and scurvy. Shackleton was particularly unwell so Scott sent him home when they finally returned to the ship. Although their public relationship remained cordial, Shackleton was hurt by the episode and became determined to salvage his pride by outdoing Scott.

He helped organise the *Discovery* relief operation but then spent several years in limbo, partly as a journalist but also as a parliamentary candidate during the 1906 General Election. He soon grew restless, however, and began making plans to return to Antarctica to reach the South Pole. Within a few months he'd secured the investment so he headed for New Zealand.

On January 1st 1908 Shackleton set sail in *Nimrod*. He'd initially promised

Scott that he wouldn't base himself at McMurdo Sound as this was Scott's territory but conditions elsewhere precluded landing so Shackleton was forced to break his agreement. The ship reached the sound on January 29th but it wasn't until October that the great southern journey began. By January 1909, Shackleton, Frank Wild, Eric Marshall and Jameson Adams had discovered the Beardmore Glacier and become the first people to map the South Polar Plateau. They also came within 112 miles of the pole itself before turning back due to starvation.

They arrived back at the ship to discover that the remaining members of the expedition had made the first ascent of Mount Erebus (the highest mountain on the continent) as well as reaching the magnetic pole. Shackleton returned home a hero and was awarded with the Royal Geographic Society's Gold Medal before receiving a knighthood from King Edward VII. Despite all the awards, the expedition returned with enormous debts and Shackleton was unable to meet the guarantees he had given his backers. So as not to denigrate the achievement, most of the debts were written off.

He then spent several years pursuing

business interests that eventually faltered so his sole source of income was from the lecture circuit. When news broke that Roald Amundsen had reached the South Pole and that Scott had died in his attempt, Shackleton initially maintained that there was no point heading south again, but he changed his mind when examining William Bruce's plans for a continental crossing from the Weddell Sea via the pole to McMurdo Sound.

It took him two years to raise the money and make preparations but *Endurance* finally left South Georgia in December 1914. As the ship moved into the Weddell Sea, it became trapped in the ice, where it would remain until November 1915. The ice had compromised its structure in the winter and it eventually sank. Shackleton and his team camped on the ice for two months but were unable to reach land and extra provisions. In April 1916 the ice floe began to break up so Shackleton ordered everyone into the lifeboats for the five-day trip to Elephant Island. When they landed, it was the first time they'd stood on solid ground for 16 months.

With the mission abandoned, the priority now lay with getting everyone home safely, and Shackleton was a fine leader who lived every moment with his men. Elephant Island was nowhere near the shipping lanes so the only hope of rescue lay with a small team making a 750-mile open-water journey in one of the lifeboats to the whaling stations on South Georgia.

Shackleton took up the challenge himself, choosing his crew based upon experience and knowledge, and setting off in the 20-foot boat in April 1916. They battled the extreme seas and hurricane-force winds of the Southern Ocean for two weeks before finally landing on the barren west coast of South Georgia. It was one of the finest feats of seamanship yet recorded. Rather than risk putting back to sea to circumnavigate the island, Shackleton, Frank Worsley and Tom Crean crossed the mountains in 36 hours and finally arrived in Stromness on May 20th.

Shackleton immediately organised rescue parties for the men stranded on Elephant Island as well as the crew of the Ross Sea party at Cape Evans in McMurdo Sound. He accomplished the former in August 1916 before heading back south to collect the remaining men in Antarctica. They had laid all their food depots across the ice as instructed but three lives had been lost.

Shackleton finally made it home in 1917 after one of the most extraordinary expeditions of all time. Although the continental crossing had failed spectacularly, the evacuation from the *Endurance*, the boat journey to Elephant Island, the arduous navigation across the Southern Ocean to South Georgia, and then the risky crossing of the island's mountains to reach civilisation is still regarded as one of the most incredible and courageous achievements in human history. To then insist upon returning to rescue all of his men personally defines Shackleton as a man.

The price he paid was heavy, however. It was thought that his heart was failing when he was sent home from Scott's expedition, and it finally gave out on South Georgia during a final ill-conceived voyage south in January 1922. His wife, Emily, asked that he be buried on the island, and there can be no more fitting place of rest than on a lonely island surrounded by stormy seas, the scene of his greatest triumph.

Above: *The lifeboat James Caird is launched from Elephant Island before its epic 750-mile journey across the Southern Ocean to South Georgia*

Sir Henry Morton Stanley, & Dr David & Mrs Mary Livingstone

Sir Henry Morton Stanley was born John Rowlands in Wales in January 1841. He endured a torrid childhood that saw him abandoned in infancy by his mother, Elizabeth Parry, and then lose his father. He was initially brought up by his grandfather, Moses Parry, but he died when John was five. The youngster ended up being abused in the St Asaph workhouse before eventually leaving at 15.

Three years later, Rowlands travelled to the United States in search of a better future. He was hired as a working boy by a wealthy but childless trader called Henry Stanley and he soon took his employer's name. He fought for the Confederacy in the American Civil War before being captured and forced to fight for the Union. He was discharged due to illness but then joined the navy as a record-keeper in 1864.

At the end of the war, Stanley became a freelance journalist and organised an expedition to the Ottoman Empire. Newspaper magnate James Gordon Bennett heard of his exploits and recruited him to the *New York Herald*. In 1869, Stanley approached Bennett and his son and asked them if he could mount a mission to find the missing missionary David Livingstone. The pair agreed to finance the expedition to Africa so Stanley left for Zanzibar in 1871.

David Livingstone was born in March 1813 in Blantyre, Scotland, to Neil and Agnes. From the age of 10 he worked in the local mill, but he then attended Charing Cross Medical School. During his formative years he developed a fascination with both science and religion and became convinced that the two could co-exist peacefully. When he heard an anti-slavery lecture he applied to join the London Missionary Society and, having been accepted, lobbied to be posted to China.

The outbreak of the First Opium War forced him to reconsider and, despite initially intending to head for the West Indies, he chose South Africa on the advice of fellow missionary Robert Moffat. He soon became convinced that slavery could be stopped by the spread of Christianity and legitimate trade. During his time in South Africa, Livingstone was attacked by a lion that left his left arm disabled for life.

Livingstone then explored much of Central Africa, becoming the first European to see Victoria Falls. Between 1854 and 1856 he undertook one of the first crossings of the continent, from Luanda on the Atlantic coast to Quelimane on the Indian Ocean. His success as a

missionary and explorer was largely due to the small size, friendly nature and lack of threat from his party. Larger European expeditions were heavily armed and were

Above: *Sir Henry Morton Stanley in 1872*

often perceived as slave-raiding parties so they were often attacked themselves. Livingstone remained approachable and cordial and he never forced the local chiefs to adopt his message.

Having seen its devastating effects firsthand, the abolition of the slave trade became his primary motivation. He believed that this could only be achieved by navigating the Zambezi so that Christianity could be spread throughout the interior and legitimate trade with African tribes would usurp the slave trade.

The Zambezi exploration mission began in 1858 and, although it achieved several notable firsts and was a scientific success, Livingstone was criticised for his poor leadership and organisation, as well as his inability to act on sound advice. Having reached and partially explored Lake Malawi, the expedition returned to the coast to take delivery of a steamboat designed to navigate the lake.

Mary Livingstone hadn't been able to join her husband on the first leg of the journey because she had been overseeing their children's schooling in Britain, but she arrived in Africa in 1862 for the second trip to the largely unchartered interior.

Mary was the daughter of Robert

Moffat and his wife, Mary Smith. She was born in Griquatown to the north of Kimberley in South Africa in 1821. Having moved to Britain for several years, the family returned to South Africa in 1843. Mary took up a teaching post in Kuruman, which is where she met her husband. The couple married two years later and she accompanied him on two trips across the Kalahari in 1849 and 1850, during which her husband had to deliver two of their six children. She returned to Africa after the children had been schooled but she then fell pregnant again before the first Zambezi expedition. Having returned to Kuruman to have the child, she rejoined Livingstone at the mouth of the Zambezi before the second mission to explore Lake Malawi. Before leaving, she fell ill and died of malaria in April 1862 at the age of only 41. She was buried in Chupanga in Mozambique.

Livingstone's second foray to Lake Malawi was hindered by poor navigation along the River Ruvuma. Their progress was further hampered when the bodies of slaves thrown into the river by traders fouled the paddlewheels. Two years later, the expedition was branded a failure and called off.

In 1866 Livingstone somehow secured funds to sponsor an expedition to find the source of the Nile. He immediately ran into problems, however, when his assistants deserted after stealing his supplies. He was eventually forced to rely on the hated Arab slave traders for help, and he reached Lake Mweru in November 1867. While wandering the jungle around the Lualaba River he became ill and again had to rely on medicines from the traders. Now suffering from pneumonia, cholera and tropical ulcers, he reached Ujiji only to find his remaining supplies had also been stolen. When he saw 400 Africans being slaughtered by slave traders in 1871, he was too horrified to continue and abandoned his expedition to find the source of the Nile. For most of the last five years Livingstone had been completely cut off from the outside world and only one of his letters home was delivered.

Stanley, meanwhile, had the financial backing to mount an enormous search operation. However, despite hiring 200 porters, his 700-mile trek through the tropics soon turned sour. His horse died after being bitten by a tsetse fly and his porters deserted when they realised how brutal a taskmaster he could be: Stanley allegedly shot several locals to maintain

Opposite: *David Livingstone*

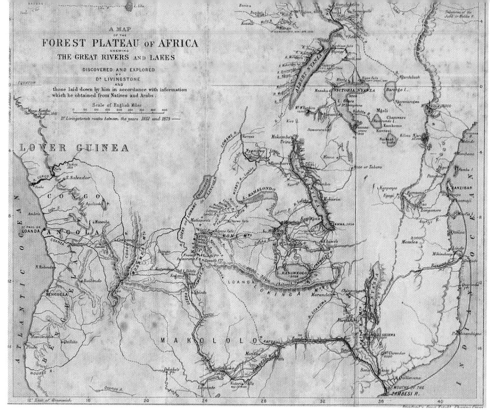

A MAP
of the
FOREST PLATEAU of AFRICA
shewing
THE GREAT RIVERS and LAKES
DISCOVERED AND EXPLORED
by
Dr LIVINGSTONE
AND
those laid down by him in accordance with information
which he obtained from Natives and Arabs.

Scale of English Miles

Dr Livingstone's routes between the years 1851 and 1873 ——

Above:

Livingstone's travels in Africa

discipline within their ranks.

He eventually tracked Livingstone down in Ujiji in November 1871. Whether or not he greeted him with the words "Dr Livingstone, I presume?" is open to debate as Stanley tore the relevant pages from his diary and Livingstone never mentioned the phrase. The *New York Times* published the line in July 1872, although it could have been invented as a humorous quip because Livingstone was the only other white man for hundreds of miles.

The two men did finally establish that there was no connection between the Nile and Lake Tanganyika but Livingstone was

by then too ill to continue his hunt for the source. He returned to Lake Bangweulu in present-day Zambia and died in May 1873 from a variety of ailments. Although he apparently converted only one man to Christianity (Sechele, chief of Botswana's Kwena people), his travels opened up Africa's heart to missionaries and colonial powers. His compassion led to Europeans opting to help the African people rather than enslaving them, and he inspired a change in mindset that challenged the belief that the Empire had the right to rule so-called lesser races.

Stanley, on the other hand, continued exploring with an iron fist. For two and a half years he charted the Congo River to the sea, although only 114 of his party of 356 survived. He was then hired by King Leopold II of Belgium to rescue Emin Pasha, Governor of Equitoria, from Sudan, although the main mission was clearly to claim more land for Belgium in the Scramble for Africa. The awful brutality of some of his party further tarnished his reputation, although that didn't stop him becoming MP for Lambeth North in 1895 and receiving a knighthood in 1899. He died in London in May 1904 and was later said to be the inspiration for the Joseph Conrad book *Heart of Darkness*.

Dame Freya Stark

Freya Stark was born in Paris in 1893 to artists Flora and Robert. She spent her formative years travelling with the family in Italy, but, when she fell ill, she found solace in reading about the Orient. She had an accident in a factory when she was just 13, which left her slightly disfigured but she learned Latin, Arabic and Persian while recuperating. Having studied at the University of London, she served with an ambulance unit during the First World War.

By 1927 she was determined to explore the Far East so she first visited Lebanon and Iraq, which was then a British protectorate. For the next three years she trekked throughout the Middle East, becoming the first Westerner into the wildernesses of central Iran and to the Valley of the Assassins. She also explored more of southern Arabia than anyone before her and then published accounts of her travels in four books.

During the Second World War, Stark joined the Ministry of Information and spent time in Syria trying to convince the Arab nations to either remain neutral or join the Allies. She married historian Stewart Perowne in 1947 but the couple separated after five years so Stark resumed her travels, first in Turkey and then in Central Asia, China, the Himalayas and finally Afghanistan. Indeed she was still trekking and writing into her 80s, although she eventually returned to Asolo in northern Italy to reflect on a life well lived.

When she died in 1993 at the age of 100, she left behind a vast body of important work chronicling the lives of the peoples of the Middle East. *The Valleys of the Assassins* (1934) and *The*

Southern Gates of Arabia (1936) are not only tales of exploration in lands not seen by Europeans but also engaging accounts of her relationships with the local people, and they are rightly acknowledged as classic works of non-fiction.

Above: *Dame Freya Stark*

Abel Tasman

Abel Tasman was born in Lutjegast in the Netherlands in 1603 but he lived an unremarkable early life until he joined the Dutch East India Company (VOC) at the age of 30 and went to Jakarta. He returned home after four years and married, but he then rejoined the VOC and was commissioned to explore the northern Pacific under Captain Matthijs Quast.

In 1642, the Council of the Indies asked Tasman and Franchoijs Visscher to map the vast continent that was thought to exist to the south of the Malaysian Peninsula (this land existed on maps drawn by Abraham Ortelius and Jan Huygen van Linschoten, but it was inaccurate and incomplete, as were the earlier maps of Marco Polo and Henricus Martellus). The land, known variously as Boeach, Locach and Terra Australis, was said to be rich in gold so there was plenty of incentive to claim it for Holland.

Tasman left for Mauritius in September 1642. There he restocked the ships – *Engel* and *Gracht* – and made the necessary repairs using the island's plentiful supply of timber. Poor weather forced Tasman to take a northerly route across the Indian Ocean but he eventually sighted Tasmania in November (he named it Van Diemen's Land). Having mapped much of the coast, he claimed the land for the Dutch in December.

He then planned to head north towards the continent thought to exist between Tasmania and Malaysia but the winds carried him east to New Zealand, which he thought must be part of South America. He mapped the coast of the South Island for five days but his boats were then attacked by Maori, which left

Left: *Abel Tasman*

four of his crew dead. He then headed north to the Tongan archipelago and Fiji in early 1643 but almost lost his ships on reefs. Having then charted Vanua Levu, he turned northwest and reached Jakarta in June via New Guinea.

The following year he took three ships – *Limmen*, *Zeemeeuw* and *Braek* – east from New Guinea but he failed to chart the Torres Strait between New Guinea and Australia, thereby missing what would become an important trading route. He mapped much of the north coast of Australia, however, and made careful observations about the land christened New Holland and its indigenous people. The Dutch East India Company remained sceptical about his achievements, however, and maintained that he'd discovered nothing of any real value. He died in Jakarta in October 1659.

The pictures in this book were provided courtesy of the following:

WIKICOMMONS
commons.wikimedia.org

Design & Artwork by Scott Giarnese

Published by Demand Media Limited

Publishers: Jason Fenwick & Jules Gammond

Written by Liam McCann